Manifest
Change

Happy Publishing

Manifest Change
Compiled and Edited by Erica Glessing

FIRST EDITION
ISBN 978-0-9895554-4-9

Cover Design by Blue Zoo Creative
Interior Design by BookPublishingMentor.com

Published by Happy Publishing, distributed by Ingram
HappyPublishing@gmail.com

Happy Publishing

Dear Reader,

I teach happiness, and this gives me joy. The years I went through a divorce, I felt upside down and inside out. I no longer knew who I was, although I loved the joy that coursed through my veins at being free from a relationship that was over.

As I went through the downs and amazing ups of finding my own space again, I felt transformation in every part of my being down to the toes of my cellular level and up into the heavens where I connect to all that is. I lost about 45 pounds, walking and being in my own zone. I became friends with light bringers who had not noticed me before. I began to feel sexy again, for the first time in 20 years. I put pen to the paper on a new book called "Happiness Quotations 365."

My intention in releasing this book is to help you experience massive transformation. As I did, and continue to do in the new space of my spirit expansion.

Finances took a turn through the changes as I stepped into supporting myself alone for the first time in two decades. Before I was married, I had my parents. Since that time, my mom passed and my dad went into care. So you're going to see some chapters in this book about finances and abundance that you might not have expected in a book about manifesting change.

I brought in some amazing finance and abundance teachers to bring light in this area.

Most of all, each author chosen for this book is dedicated to helping people change. This book resonates with complete authenticity as each and every author – all of whom I have grown to love – is committed personally to be the change they want to see in the world. I brought in happiness experts, health and healing experts, personal potential experts, and possibly the very message you need right now to shift your life to the next level.

A special note: the authors are from all around the globe. I have left in their native spellings so the word "favorite" might be "favourite" in New Zealand or Australia. Just as an observation, each author's native English was the spelling I allowed for each of the chapters.

I am grateful and joyful that this book is now moving into your hands. If it does anything to change your life please send me a note. I know I can speak for my fabulous authors when I say that we care about you.

Sincerely,

Erica

Erica M. Glessing
HappyPublishing@gmail.com

Table of Contents

CHAPTER 1

We Change as We Desire

By *Thomas Weatherspoon*
Master Trainer

In the process of trying to make a transformation, one must first be inspired to take the necessary steps toward the idea. It is never practical to move without inspiration. Over the 28 years that I have been working in the field of high performance training, I have come to recognize that it is the inspired idea that is the cause of most successful transformations. Without the inspiration the journey is simply moved by a goal, something we want or wish for.

Goals take motivation to keep one moving in the direction of accomplishment. There is a very powerful difference between motivation and inspiration. Motivation is encouragement, and may come from another individual. Inspiration, on the other hand, is something more compelling because it comes from within.

An inspiration, according to the dictionary, is a process, a quality, an idea, a breath or a divine influence. What is not expressed in that notion is the sense that it must be, that the process has to be initiated, the quality has to be expressed, and the idea's time has come. Just like breathing, it is necessary for our survival. It is that sense of pure fact or demand of expression that makes the inspiration far more influential than motivation.

As a Master Trainer there is far less mental work to be done with an inspired client, versus someone who is goal-oriented.

It is this sense of clarity, or the inner knowledge of the inspired idea, that shapes our desire. In this process of opening to and trusting our inner voice, we find that the intuitive commands resonate so perfectly because they are harmonious with our entire being. Whereas choosing a goal before being intuitively inspired is simply a wish or a want and usually comes with some anxiety or angst about its accomplishment. This tends to be the case because it is ego-based and attached to a particular outcome.

The wishes or wants of the ego are rarely a point in the right direction of one's divine purpose.

It is so easy these days to group desire, goal, inspiration, want or wish together but, nothing could be further from the truth energetically or emotively. In most cases the person being driven by their desire (an intuitively inspired idea), have resolved themselves to the task of bringing it into fruition. In my experience it is these individuals that have what we call in the industry, Heart! When clients walked through the door of our facility I welcomed each one by saying, "We don't make Hearts here, Heart you must bring through the door with you." Heart represented the quality, reflective of the individual that was inspired to be accomplished from deep within. This kind of person simply needed guidance on their journey and was dedicated to the task from the inception of the idea.

I have worked with so many who have trained hard to achieve an ego-based goal and used as their motivation, wealth, position or fame. In the end, regardless of their success, the pursuit of such an endeavor brought with it an uneasiness and more problems. The difficulty is in finding a goal that will bring to our lives a sense of harmony and peace. We can't be sure that the accomplishment of our goal is going to make us truly happier though we believe it will. That's why I encourage you to be divinely inspired and wait on your trusted guide to lead you toward the next level. It is only through the yearning of the inner voice's knowing that we are put on the path to magic. This magic creates balance, peace and harmony in our lives.

In the fall of 2012 I returned home to Milwaukee from a visit in California. At a family Gathering, I met a young woman by the name of Terri M. She was a heavy-set, attractive person, in both looks and personality. She was intelligent, funny and quite personable. She was from the south originally and had a strong southern accent. As the night went on everyone in my family pulled me to the side one after another to ask if I would help Terri with her weight problem because in their eyes she was one of the most darling people they had ever met. My curiosity was peaked. How had this woman made such an impression on my entire family?

Over the course of the night, Terri and I got a chance to speak, and we talked about actually getting together the next day to go for a walk. We agreed to meet at the lakefront on Milwaukee's East side. The next day we met and began walking at a slow enough pace so we could have a normal conversation. During that conversation I learned of Terri's many health problems associated with her weight. Terri was 348 pounds and stood about 5′5 inches. As well as being overweight, Terri also had MS, Diabetes and high blood pressure. I was shocked to say the least but the more we walked the more I learned of her life. There were issues with the last few failed relationships in her life. She was constantly being taken advantage of for her giving nature. Men seemingly only wanted money or sex. After only a two-mile walk and lots of talking and crying, Terri agreed to work with me for the next month so we could find her inspiration.

We met every day at the same time to walk. We started

with just two miles and eventually worked our way up to seven- and eight-mile walks on some days. We moved through all of the collective memories of her pain and searched for that small voice that was being drowned out by her connection to it.

Terri began verbalizing out loud her inner voices desires. She was reluctant because she didn't believe she could physically get better, so that she might achieve some of them.

We changed her eating habits along the way so she would not take into her system more negativity. Once she began acknowledging her voice she ended the destructive relationships in her life. As she put it, "She started letting go of the toads in her life, though there were one or two frogs she would still have to deal with."

Our walks were filled with laughter and optimism. By the month's end Terri had dropped 48 pounds, more than ever before. Her health had improved through the healthier eating plan and exercise. She had proven to herself that she could make this change. I pointed out to her, as there are no accidents in the universe, she began making the change the moment she said yes to its' possibility.

Terri is healthier and happier today and continues to break barriers as she creates the life she was destined for by following her small voice of desire. We are all looking for the "more" we could be: healthier, wealthier, and happier. But it is not the ego that we can trust when making it happen.

A quote often attributed to Albert Einstein says "The intuitive mind is a sacred gift and the rational mind is a faithful servant. We have created a society that has honored the servant and forgotten the gift." Our intuitive minds speak to us in the language we call desire and moves us toward our divine purpose. The purpose that represents the blueprint formed for us at the point of our creation. The gift is in the unknown peace, harmony and balance that comes with following your divine direction.

ABOUT THE AUTHOR: *Thomas Weatherspoon*

Thomas Weatherspoon, Master Trainer, has been transforming lives for a long time. His High Performance Training program has been improving performances of Professional Athletes, Olympians, artists, educators, CEO's, movie stars, singers and more for over 28 years.

He is a professional trainer, athlete, poet, spiritual mentor and speaker. He has a rare ability to inspire and coach a person beyond his or her perceived limitations and to bring them into a profound relationship with their spirit. His accomplishments have been noted in magazines, on television and newspapers worldwide.

He has two companies, PEPA Sports and Path to Magic. He is the author of five books of poetry and *Path to Magic – The 19 Principles of Transformation*. His latest book, a children's book, *Professor Finds His Path*, is also a full curriculum used in schools within the United States. His online course; "Finding Your Divine Purpose," has helped people from all walks of life and parts of the world and is prepped for publishing in 2014. Find out more at www.ThomasWeatherspoon.com.

Chapter 2

Manifest Your Life's Dream

By Bec Robbins

We dream, each one of us. Not just in sleep, but every day in our wakened state. We dream of what we'd REALLY like to do, what we'd really like to have, who we'd really like to be with.

In essence, our dreams are a collection of desires.

Even when we have a life brimming with blessings and gratitude, **somewhere within us is a whisper for more.** For different. For greater. For brighter. Yet many of us chide ourselves for wanting more. We are encouraged to be at peace with what we have, to accept our realities and concede to what is, to surrender our desires and simply be.

It is counter intuitive to regard our dreams and desires for what they really are: **a call to evolve our souls.** For our dreams do not come from within us. They come THROUGH us from a source much more vast and infinite than ourselves.

They come from the source of all things, the Universe itself. **Our dreams are in effect, divine forces that pull us forward into expansion.** They are held before us like a cosmic, dangling carrot that we are meant to reach for. But to grasp, we must become who we are not yet. We must grow into a higher version of ourselves, a refined expression of our soul.

Personal evolution is required to grasp our dreams. And personal evolution is also the fundamental contribution we owe to human consciousness. For that reason alone, **grasping our dreams is our cosmic moral obligation.** Not selfish, not indulgent, but mandatory for our highest good and the good of all.

The more dreams we successfully transform into realities, the more evolved we automatically become. And the more evolved we become, the more capacity we have to impact the world as a whole and improve the Universe at large. This is the common charge the Universe has given us all.

With this charge **we are also given everything we need to be successful in realizing our dreams.** The Universe will not activate a desire within us if we do not already have the ability to grasp it. The task falls on us then, to become both aware and willing.

We must cultivate awareness of the yet unseen resources available to us and also muster the willingness to do what it takes to become who we must in order to receive what we desire.

At all costs; despite fears, failures, resistances and obstacles, we must commit to crafting our dreams into realities because **by not achieving our dreams we are doing our souls, the world and the cosmos at large a great disservice!**

How then, do we realize and manifest our dreams? Acknowledgement of the above truth is the first step because it shifts our perspective from judging our dreams as self-indulgent or unrealistic to holding them reverent. We can begin to give ourselves permission to prioritize our burning desires as something of extreme importance, not just for the Self but for all.

Without this permission the steps of manifesting our dreams can become arduous and the co-creative journey can be plagued with discouragement. This is when we give up on dreams and thus give up on our soul's contribution. **We must know deeply the importance and value of our dreams to be successful in manifesting them.**

Before we delve into the essential steps required to transform dreams into realities, it is also important to understand what lies at the innermost core of all of our desires. Understanding our root motivations will help us more easily evolve in order to grasp our dreams. Working with people to realize their dreams for over a decade, and fine tuning my own process to make real my desires has exposed to me **two core elements that awaken all desires within us.**

Underneath all the themes of what we desire; more wealth, more health, more love and more meaning to name the most common, lie two very specific experiential traits. These traits emerge as a pattern when asking various subjects one key question: **WHY do you want what you want?**

And not just asking once but asking, "Why" again and again to trace the desire to its core.

This distillation of a desire is like dropping into a rabbit hole that leads to one if not both of two chambers.

The two things at the root of all desire are FREEDOM and/or FULFILLMENT.

We are most deeply motivated to experience freedom to be who we really are, to express and have choice. We crave freedom from pain, fear, struggle and suffering.

As well our motivation to desire lies in a sense of fulfillment: of our purpose and calling, of our hearts, minds and bodies. One can argue that fulfillment is essentially freedom from void and that freedom is simply fulfillment of infinite possibility. But each (and sometimes both) makes a distinct appearance at the root of the great majority of our human desires.

Take a moment now to consider your most burning desire and ask yourself, "why" and then "why" again and again and you will come to one if not both of these root desires.

These are the king and queen of evolutionary forces: the two experiential Holy Grails that we are all after. Knowledge of this truth helps us realize our dreams more effectively because we can then already embody these core experiences well before grasping our desire.

And in embodying the energies of **freedom and fulfillment consistently we become more magnetic to the resources, guidance and support required to manifest our divine dreams.**

Now let's return to the question of how.

How do we manifest and realize our dreams? How do we achieve the deep freedom and fulfillment that is associated with our desires?

As mentioned before, we already have the capacity and ability to do so, but we have forgotten.

This "forgetting" is intrinsic in our evolutionary process. **We do in fact forget by design, as per our soul's pre-prescribed path.** It is in this temporary ignorance of our capabilities that we gain vital wisdom and learning that will play a key role in our awakened or "remembering" chapter of life. There comes, for those called and willing, an awakening or re-learning of our ability to manifest our desires.

Some of us awaken to this early in life and others quite late, yet others who do not awaken in this lifetime at all. **If you are reading these words right now there is a good chance you have already awakened, you are awakening right now or you are about to awaken to the truth of your abilities to manifest.**

These abilities can be classified into three main categories. They are, in effect, three distinct skill sets that, once mastered, **enable one to evolve and thus manifest ANY dream into a reality.**

The first skill is the ability to self-heal. Not to heal in the sense of fixing things broken or ill but rather heal in the sense of releasing that which we are not; that which impedes us and shrouds us from our innate power and wisdom. This healing includes primarily **the ability to release all false or limiting beliefs that feed our thought patterns with illusory content.** This is most important because what we believe is what we perceive. It is a common misconception that we must first see it to believe it, but in truth we must believe what we wish to see.

This healing also includes the **release of pent up emotional energy currents.** Emotional energy that is left unexpressed is a tangible force within us. Like a live wire, it is perceived by the brain as an internal threat. The presence of such a force triggers fear and anxiety on an instinctual level, which distorts our perception and behavior in ways that sabotage our efforts to manifest our dreams.

Another area of required healing is around our **"pattern of relating."** This pattern describes the way we have learned to give and receive energy in all forms from all people, places and things. Manifesting our desires depends on a balanced exchange of energy between us and all aspects of the Universe. If our pattern of relating is not healthy, we are unable to shape and shift energy ample towards manifesting our dreams.

The second skill is the ability to reveal and align with the truth. This includes the truth of who we are, the truth of why we are here and what our soul is here to create, the truth of our conditions and environments, Universal energetic truths and so forth. It is the ability to consistently separate what is true from what is false; what is creative from what is destructive. For where there is truth, there is love. And where there is love, there is infinite creative potential and power.

The third skill, building on the second, is the ability to consciously co-create our realities as a reflection of the truth of who we are and why we are here. Conscious co-creation is fundamentally the ability to move and shape both seen and unseen energy to form something three-dimensionally. In other words, make real a desire or dream. Co-creation involves collaboration; working energetically in tandem with others, including the Universe. It requires the ability to execute both the masculine and feminine aspects of the co-creative process. The masculine aspect is the planning and physical action necessary and the feminine aspect is the attraction and magnetizing of resources using personal energy management tools.

Within these three skill sets are a number of various practices that are each themselves a topic for a chapter in this book. Examples of these practices include intuitive development, purpose exploration and discovery, personal frequency management, intentional living, mindset correction, and mastering energy exchange.

Although the details of these processes are not included in this chapter, what is most important to note is that none of these practice or skills are considered rocket science. None require a specific degree of education or any advanced knowledge. **The attainment of these skills requires two things: belief and persistence.** We require belief in our ability to manifest our dreams and persistence to break our old constructs and patterns to make way for a new way of being and creating.

With belief and persistence the study, practice and application of these skills becomes enjoyable, empowering and life changing. **They enable each of us to manifest our authentic divine desires and propel our souls toward their highest possible version.**

We owe it to ourselves, to the world and to the Universe to master these skills and lead by example, teaching others how to manifest alongside us. **This is how we sustain our deepest freedom and fulfillment in this lifetime and beyond.** This is how we live our full potential. This is how we leave our greatest cosmic legacy.

ABOUT THE AUTHOR: *Bec Robbins*

Bec Robbins is a personal success coach who specializes in helping people fulfill their life's purpose and co-create lives that are rooted in deep freedom and fulfillment.

After a marriage and career breakdown coupled with a health scare in 2010, Bec discovered her own life's purpose and divine gift to guide people home to their authentic selves and empower them to co-create their deepest desires. She now has a thriving coaching practice and teaches her My Mandala™ Manifestation Living System to clients and coaches worldwide awakening the inherent creative power we each have to forge our individual realities. Bec currently resides in North Vancouver, British Columbia, Canada with her daughter Meelah.

For free resources please visit www.becrobbins.com or join the Bec Robbins Facebook Community. Contact Bec directly at bec@becrobbins.com.

Chapter 3

trans•for•ma•tion
(trănsfôr-māsh-en)

By Pascale Battrick

n.
1. The act or an instance of transforming.
2. A marked change, as in appearance or character, usu-
ally for the better.
3. A metamorphosis during the life cycle of an animal.

When I think of the word "transformation" I immediately picture two things happening: a caterpillar changing into a butterfly and a rock of carbon changing into a diamond. In both cases, neither will ever return to the thing it was before. Both the caterpillar and the carbon were destined to become something more, something greater, a more complex system and undoubtedly far superior in their attractiveness, richness and inherent value as a result of their enduring hardship or pressure. When

I consider the human race in the same regard, I see the value in struggle and perturbation because that is the point at which growth and achievement in this life and the next occurs. I see a purpose for my striving for excellence in all things, for seeking balance in life, for taking risks and challenging myself, for desiring something more than what I have created for myself and for reaching my threshold so that I might break through and break free, instead of breaking down.

I've always been a person who wanted to be liked by others. I never wanted to disappoint anyone and lived only to please. Throughout my youth, I had many friends and was trusted by teachers, co-workers and employers. I was blessed with a loving family, wonderful friends, a fruitful education and the ability to travel the world in search of that sense of self that was not inherently lost, though was not yet visible to me. I remember wanting to leave my paradise not because I was unhappy or unfulfilled, but because I wanted to explore what this world had to offer, and I felt an unquenchable desire to know my rightful place in it.

I embarked upon a journey that I'd intended to last 15 months, but which ended up spanning 15 years. I said goodbye to all that I knew and put all my faith in the uncertain. I was excited and I felt free. Even at that early and tender age I knew an innate truth - that I was freedom girl. My highest value was freedom, in all its forms. Nevertheless, it would take me over a decade to discover what my sense of freedom truly looked and felt like, and the journey towards it was destined to be one filled with tumult and sadness, victory and joy, friendship and love, spirit and connection, and unbridled transformation.

At that time I was well and truly an extroverted introvert, which meant that I had an abundance of energy and positivity for others and barely any for myself, because inside, I was a frightened little girl with a don't-shine-the-spotlight-on-me attitude. That was the person I buried deep inside and never showed anyone, not even myself, because she made me feel afraid, ignorant, worthless, useless, unwanted, unloved, undervalued and lowly. At a very early age I learnt to build a brick wall around that girl, gradually and over a long time, almost imperceptibly, so as to not allow my conscious self to become aware and reveal that girl outwardly. I chose a false sense of safety and security as her blanket, then put on a face of pure joy and happiness and a costume of unlimited positive energy so that my outer world always reflected love and light and laughter. I delved into a life of serving others, always giving one hundred percent of my time and energy to their cause so that they might prosper and grow and that I might be acknowledged one day as being useful, wanted and liked in this world. That would be my place - I would be a living martyr. It was a good plan, or so I thought.

I ventured across the oceans to the other side of the world in search of something greater than the life I was living, not knowing what was before me. I went first to France whose beautiful language and culture was not my own. I struggled to find the courage to speak up and show my capabilities because I felt invisible to these people. My feelings of inadequacy consumed me and within a matter of days I had succumbed to the abyss of my own sadness and fear, and left the country an inconsolable and weakened mess. I took myself to England and set about finding work and making friends. I was so incredibly afraid of venturing out, afraid of myself and of failure that even my relatives who had taken me in thought me somewhat out of my depth. With time, I did end up finding work and I did make friends. I travelled around Western Europe on my own and carved out my path back to France. A year later to the day, I returned there a changed woman, a more adventurous and seemingly more fearless woman with a carefree attitude and a sense of faith in my destiny to do well.

I took a job in a hotel kitchen where no English was spoken except by the Dutchman who owned the hotel and the foreign tourists who'd swarm in during the summer months. That was a safe enough move for me because all I had to do was watch and learn. For two whole weeks I said nothing. I simply observed. I discovered that the French language that I had learned at school did not serve me as well as I'd expected in France as it was all so "textbook". The French didn't seem to speak that way and whenever I'd start a sentence, they'd finish it before the words had even formed in my mouth. As time went by I relaxed, opened up and soaked up the culture, language and lifestyle like a sponge. Within the year I was fluent in the language and running the kitchen on my own with no worries. I had become *"Pascalou, la petite cheffette."* I was respected by my co-workers and the customers and I had been welcomed in by the people there like a new-found family member. The locals trusted me with their secrets, their stories and their woes. I was seen as someone from whom they could seek advice without receiving any judgment or unkind regards. At that time I did wonder why people twice my age would ask me for advice about overcoming alcoholism, rebuilding relationships, living a spiritual life, being positive on a daily basis, and how to run their businesses better. What did I know? Perhaps my job then was just to listen. Again, clarity would remain lost on me until many, many years later.

I spent a total of two and a half years in Europe, travelling to different countries and stopping for a few months to work when I'd run out of money. I always had just enough to live the life I was enjoying and I always had everything I needed. I made friends easily and I was now a French-trained chef, and that made me feel like I'd accomplished something great. Nevertheless, there lived deep inside of me a dissatisfaction with how "useful" I was being to the world. It was at this time that the Twin Towers were brought down and I felt a need to return home to "settle" a bit and get serious about life. I knew that my new skills would serve me well and the new level of understanding of the world helped me to form a fascination with global politics, the environment and conflict resolution on a grand scale. The choice was to return to New Zealand and do some formal studies so that I might find a job in something that would change this place for the better. That thought made me feel useful and worthy of these new bounties I'd been given, and so I made that long trip home, filled with hope and excitement and a new vision for my life.

I took up a chef job part-time and entered university to learn the ins and outs of international relations and politics, conflict resolution and disarmament, super soldiers and nanotechnology, all whilst studying three languages: French, Japanese and Spanish. I thought I would become the ultimate international peace-maker, seeing as that was the role I had aimed to play in all my other social and professional circles. Once I had graduated I immediately returned to Europe, spending another year or so cooking up a storm in France and travelling to parts of the Middle East and Eastern Europe. I ended up back in London too, working for a government department and truly believing that I would make a difference in policy with my new age ideals and dedication to bringing about unity and advancement in the world around me.

However, the novelty of big city life wore thin rather quickly. I was in the corporate world, commuting with lifeless bodies from stop A to stop B, eating foods that came pre-seasoned, pre-heated, and pre-packaged, in boxes and bags and trays. I trained myself to get up an hour earlier than the rest of the world just so that I could get a seat on the train and leave the office early enough to still see some daylight. The grey skies and grey faces I saw day in and out became my new normal. There did exist some life and excitement in London, certainly, it's just that it was not enough a part of my daily routine.

I had a wonderful community of friends outside of work, with whom I could grow myself spiritually and for whom I would sacrifice my evenings and weekends just to be around and to share energy and space. I also got healthier in the second year - that extra 10-15 kilos of what is known as "the Heathrow injection", started to fall away as I began making my own healthy work lunches and training in a Brazilian martial art known as Capoeira (the only form of exercise I enjoyed at that time). Yet even my hobbies, which began as a choice, a fun session once or twice a week, became somewhat of an obligation with eight classes a week, of which two were me stepping in as the instructor. Again I could not say no. Again I filled my hours with the lives of others. No space or peace was wholly mine. At that time I was ignorant to that truth because the little girl inside of me was locked far away and so I continued to do all that I could to fill up my days with what I truly thought and felt was me living the dream, in my silent pursuit to be liked, valued and seen.

As for my belief that I could create positive change within an environment as toxic as the political realm, well, that was never going to happen. It was a beast with several heads and a grip that sapped the energy and zeal out of its workers and gave way to backbiting, gossip and a malfunctioning of the wheel of life. I did enjoy the (misconceived) high esteem of being a public servant living in the big smoke, yet at the same time I was slowly burning my life-candles at both ends, falling terribly ill every three months like clockwork, staying up all hours writing and producing for other people's deadlines and working so hard to find those brief glimmers of downtime and sunshine that never seemed to satisfy.

I had unconsciously returned to my comfy habits of wanting to please others, never saying no, sacrificing my own sanity and growth for the sake of anyone who asked anything of me and accepting with grace whatever dollar-value my superiors instructed I was worth. After a little over three years I had climbed the corporate ladder as far as I wanted to go without getting into management, because by then I saw that life as one contrary to my own integrity and values. I decided it was time to let go of the political realm and delve into something more constructive and less soul-destroying. I made up my mind to return home again for a few months' break before heading to Japan and to try my hand at a new career, as a teacher of bright, vibrant youth. I remember the final days before my departure from the UK as being ones of pain and delusion, sickness and weakness. Not because I was sad to leave, quite the contrary. Unbeknownst to me, my burnt out body had succumbed to a bacterial chest infection and pneumonia, and as I flew the 25 or so hours across the planet to my home country, slipping in and out of consciousness, severely dehydrated and growing more and more incapable of controlling my own limbs, I had no idea that a moment of enlightenment was upon me.

I was rushed to the hospital, put into isolation with a team of eight doctors and nurses moving hastily around me, attaching tubes and machines. I don't remember much, except the thought that this could not be my end, could it? What had I achieved? Who had I helped or had a positive influence on? Had I lived my life's purpose? Even in my deluded state, the thought that I might depart this place without having achieved any great mission scared me. After two days under observation I was eventually given permission to recover at home, and it was then I chose to make a concerted effort to support myself, to focus on unearthing my true purpose and calling in life and to honour my body and spirit at the same time. It was time I learnt to say no. It was time for me to transform again - at that moment however, I just didn't know how.

There was to be a seven-month wait before I would be accepted to go to Japan. I struggled to find work for such a short period, even with the skills I had in the hospitality industry and corporate realm, no one was hiring for anything other than a permanent position. I found myself sitting in the offices of the Work and Income Department, waiting to find out if my previous tax-paying dollars would allow me a brief moment of reprieve and I'd be granted a benefit for the few remaining months before departure, simply to assist with my living costs. No, was the answer. I was entitled to a few measly dollars to go towards the board I was paying and nothing else purely because I didn't fit into the strict confines of what an unemployment beneficiary was. I also had to show up to the office three times a week to show them evidence that I was looking for work. I felt like I was back at school, but permanently in the detention room. I would go through each week, surviving on my savings and constantly scouring through the classifieds for anything suitable for a person living "in transit".

Then one day, I saw an ad for an internationally recognised fitness education program that had managed to condense six months of learning into an eight-week intensive diploma in executive personal training, group fitness instruction, nutrition and business. I couldn't believe my luck! With a professional registration that was also recognised in Australia and the UK and the ability to take my first steps to break away from the dreary nine to five rat race, it seemed worth the call.

It was going to cost me about $5,000 and operate like a job. I had to dress in corporate attire for classes, be there before 9am and stay until after 5 p.m., Monday to Friday. The rules were strict: miss a class and lose the grades, if you're late by a matter of minutes, you are sent home and lose the grades, if you're not in the proper attire, you're sent home and probably lose the grades, if you're not in the mood to participate, you're sent home and again, lose the grades. Get in, get it done and get out there, with a smile and a professional attitude. To me this was perfect. In eight short weeks I learned all I needed to know about the anatomy, about how the body responded to exercise, how to train clients from all ages and abilities, how to work with fatigue, illness, injury and so on, how to give basic nutrition advice and how to build my own business as a sole trader. I worked with such focused intensity day and night and, true to form, became everyone's friend in the process and ensured that the instructors and coaches all liked and counted on me.

The move to Japan approached and soon I was teaching English to high school students and building my health and fitness business on the side. I'd conduct women's wellness weekends with my girlfriends and teach "kiwi cooking" to the locals once a month. I loved the juxtaposition of modernity and tradition in Japan, the eclectic mix of kimonos, "salary men" and high fashion. Everything was just so perfect, clean, done the "right" way. I loved it all. Not a moment went by where I felt like my foreignness was unwelcome and I had simplified my life to such a degree that even my chickpea-sized apartment was perfect for me. When I finally made the choice to return home to New

Zealand to launch my fitness business, it felt like the simplest of decisions. I was fit, healthy, clear-headed and highly motivated to get started. It felt so right to me because I knew that I had to be my own boss - I did not fit the status quo and I was okay with that. Entrepreneurship was going to be my saving grace because I could do whatever I wanted to make my services fit to the needs of the day. My business would be organic in nature and grow with the times. I would learn new things and incorporate them into my services. Already I had plans to do a sort of "ready-steady-cook" session in the home, so that my clients could not only have high-end personal training, but also nutritious cooking instruction from a fully trained and experienced chef. There was no service like it available in my home country to my knowledge, so that would be my unique selling point.

Not three weeks after I landed on home soil my city suffered a crippling earthquake. The central business district fell apart and there was utter chaos in the streets. Because no one was killed in that first quake, we all felt such a sense of relief and with our "get on with it" attitude, the locals did just that. I launched my business immediately and took the time to volunteer as a fitness instructor for those who had learnt that walking eight hours over rubble and silt to reach their loved ones was a challenge. I felt purposeful and that I was meant to be here to take part in the rebuild. Some months later, an even worse earthquake struck, killing people and destroying any remnants of the inner city.

I remember my family and I collecting our passports and birth certificates, a clean change of clothes and a warm jacket, then shutting the door of our house as its walls crumbled to the ground and we walked away, unlikely to return. What looked like a war zone was now my new reality and yet somehow, I didn't want to abandon it, though I was encouraged to do so by my peers. I felt a pull towards helping this place to heal and I knew that the discovery of my true purpose and calling in life was close.

At the same time as building a business in an economic downturn and in a quake-torn city, I immersed myself in networking, forming new business relationships, self-study and personal development programs at home and abroad, as a means to stretch outside of my comfort zone and expand my self-concept. I realised that there was a message inside of me that wanted to come out, yet the environment in which I found myself wasn't one that was supporting my growth and transformation. I chose to travel abroad every three to six weeks to reach my breakthroughs and to get to know myself better. The end of my 15-year search for my truth and my freedom was looming and I could feel it in my bones. My friends and family were afraid for me because they knew that all this travel and change must have been costing me the earth (and believe me, it was!), but my drive and willingness to pursue what felt like an overwhelming rightness for me had me thinking "if I don't succeed, I must be dead, because there's nothing I am more passionate about than realising my truth in this life".

I made connections with people who led me to other people who then opened doors and helped me expand and grow in my business and in my self-esteem. I journeyed far and wide and built new relationships with people who would become my greatest teachers, because I would suffer my greatest losses through working with them or being close to them. One relationship in particular had brought me my highest highs and my lowest lows, both professionally and personally, because they robbed me of my gifts and did it all with an artificially warm smile and a hug, to which I flocked like a moth to a flame. The mirrors they held up to my face revealed that I was giving up my power to them, yet again, sacrificing the growth of my own business and the pursuit of my own dreams to satisfy and fulfil theirs.

Why did I do that? What was I gaining by overlooking injustice and dissatisfaction and letting the energy thieves take from me so ungraciously? At that time I naively believed that my gifts and talents wouldn't be taken for granted because I expected integrity and uprightness from them, just as I did from myself. I was also led to believe that I was going to reap some future benefit and, being recognized as a forceful leader, would join the directorship of the company. What ended up happening was I let my first business, my baby, slowly plod along, merely treading water, whilst I injected all my energy, original ideas, skills and life into someone else's dream. And they ran away with it, without paying me a dime or crediting my work. My investment in them was somewhere between $60,000 to $100,000 and, as I silently, privately, hit rock bottom, up to my ears in mounting debt, fighting a tiresome battle as my fears of failure and my insecurities about how successful I could be as an entrepreneur and businesswoman nearly consumed me, heart and soul, I experienced a nano-second of foresight.

I remember the day when I held in my left hand the option to file for bankruptcy as a simple escape, just to take away the pain of financial distress and the pressure I was under to pay everyone else but myself, and in my right hand the option to stand up, hold my head high and press onwards and upwards. Option one would take me away from my ultimate goal of freedom, which thankfully I had the foresight to see even in my grief-stricken state, and therefore was not a suitable choice for me. I chose to do one thing every day to help me build a positive relationship with money and do one other thing every day to bring me closer to my goals. One step for each was the aim and little by little, day by day, I grew and grew and grew.

It didn't take long for me to find prosperity again. It is true that my one leap of faith toward my uncertain future brought a thousand leaps from the universe toward me and my goal. Once I had learned to let go of any bitterness or grief at the loss of what could have been for me and my business partners, and once I had found gratitude for all the opportunities for growth and learning that my knowing them had brought into my life, my daily rituals of creating bite-sized goals and celebrating small successes shaped my new pathway. I attracted new people into my life who added a deep richness to the tapestry that was my reinvention, my reinvigoration and my transformation. I had reached my point of perturbation in business and self-worth: phase one. I rose up, and with "everyday in every way my life gets better and better" as my mantra and small signs as my confirmation that I was directed aright, my days became brighter and my being found its rightful place again.

My entry into phase two of my major self-transformation came with the creation of what started out as an accountability group of four friends. This group connects daily across two countries and the initial intention was simply to keep the momentum of growth going between us by way of a sacred space to share trials and triumphs and to support one another. Me and my three soul sisters are now known as the Goddesses of the Red Tent, and our sacred space has become a nexus for immense love, passion, growth, gratitude, abundance and rapid, rapid change. The energy between our four walls is unlike anything I have ever experienced before and the beauty of our team of warrior goddesses is that we embrace womanhood wholly and without fear or expectation. We do not limit ourselves to the confines that society sets up for us and we do not allow any one of us to become a victim in any way, shape or form. We are each others' mirrors, reflecting back to one another the attributes we wish to see in ourselves, as well as the self-limiting beliefs that might hold us back from succeeding as a means to highlight them for avoidance. My Red Tent ladies - Hridaya, Goddess of the Heart, Shelley, the Rainbow Lioness and Holly, our one and only Dancing Thunder - are my most ardent supporters, the blood sisters I never had, and the ones who have no agenda other than the Red Tent Agenda, which is based on a will to live abundantly, inspirationally, progressively and wholeheartedly with love.

When I share my learnings of the day within the Red Tent, my fellow goddesses open their hearts to me and do not judge. If I choose to weep, they let me weep and discourage me from repressing my emotion, to allow space for perturbation and breakthrough. If I choose to laugh and dance and sing, they join me in that joy and celebrate with me. They shine their mirrors to my face with ruthless compassion in order to guide me to finding my own truth, to learn from my tests and they too in turn, learn from the lessons I am facing as they see mirrors of their own. Together we have taught each other the intricacies of heartbreak and creating true love, of playing games of courtship and of standing in one's power when communicating matters of the heart. We have expanded our respective business ventures by using the Red Tent as a sort of board room for masterminding ideas and fleshing out the details. Those ladies, those superior beings of light and love, are a big part of the reason I am so successful. We keep each other accountable to weekly goals in business, in financial freedom and in life. We track everything that is important to us and we connect in person as often as we can. The Red Tent has its own "Code of Honour", which outlines our commitment to ourselves and each other.

We have a Red Tent Charity commitment and a special collective fund dedicated to celebrating our individual successes. We each create weekly goals, yearly goals, 5-, 10- and 30-year goals, we create annual bucket lists and support each other in achieving them, we create vision boards and experience boards together and the intense spirit, wisdom, energy and love within is something that can only be replicated by knowing what it is that we know. Perhaps that knowledge is something that the Red Tent as a whole will share with the world, in time.

Earlier in 2013 I attended a training event with my fellow goddesses to learn how to better deliver my message to the world. The phase two I spoke of previously came about at that event when I found myself faced with an ancient, well-formed, well-enforced self-limiting belief that I was not seen as someone who's energy and inherent message were much appreciated, needed or explicitly wanted. I was consciously aware that I was already living in alignment with my true purpose though, that I was valued in some small way to some people, and that my Red Tent ladies had helped me to heal my malformed belief to a degree that I couldn't have done on my own. And yet, at that event, my biggest moment of truth was upon me after having experienced several days of emotional growth and perturbation. I was invited to speak to the entire room, hundreds of people, to energise them, to build up the intensity and context of the space, to add value to them and to ensure that they, the individual audience members themselves, felt seen, wanted, needed and valued. With courage I accepted the challenge because I knew I had to do it to release that cursed self-limiting belief of mine once and for all, and to save myself.

I remember it so vividly. I was nervous, so aimed to have fun to get my own energy up. I felt the tension rising and ran around the room to get every single soul up out of their seats. I had them dancing, cheering, singing, laughing and just being free. They were mine, for a moment, and I loved them all. As my well-practiced process came to an end, I punched my fist into the air and gave a yelp of relief and elation rolled into one, because I had accomplished my most overwhelming, most outrageous task to date. Just as the main speaker came to the stage to congratulate me, the entire room erupted into a standing ovation, clapping, cheering, whistling, and shouting words of support for the gift I had just given them. I was overcome with emotion and burst into tears as I felt the energy coming from them seep into every pore and take hold of every particle within me. My arms were forced outwards as though to embrace the entire room, and my face, streaming with tears and beaming a huge smile, scanned every single loving pair of eyes looking back at me.

I stood there for what felt like an eternity, weeping from such a deep place that I can only conclude that all my fears and insecurities were leaving my body. I felt a rush of love and compassion from the crowd with such intensity that it hit me on a cellular level, affecting every part of my heart, soul and being. I knew innately that the immensity of what I was experiencing came down to one thing: this was my first conscious sense of unconditional love that I had let in, ever. I felt seen, wanted and loved and I allowed myself to embrace it. I felt as though my most important transformation to date was happening before my very eyes and I was overcome with gratitude for the opportunity and for all those people who gave back a hundredfold what I had given them. The Goddesses of the Red Tent were also there to help me physically and spiritually anchor that feeling into my very being and in that moment, I was free.

Opening the door to an inner world of which I was previously unaware really exacerbated that phase of my personal transformation and became the catalyst for an intense period of growth for me. In the four weeks after that event I closed the loop and created a life for myself that was wholly me: it was me living my truth, inspiring and empowering others to transform their lives, and I mean that in a real way, not in a wishy-washy, hippie-esque, feel-good way, because the people entering my sphere genuinely are changing their lives for the better through working with me, and that in turn reinforces my belief in my purpose and encourages me to continue my good work. I am open to new adventures and the opportunities for even further learning and growth are ever present. I am at another rung on my life ladder and even though what is behind me is what has made me, what is before me is only coming because of who I choose to be today and who I will choose to become tomorrow, and my options are innumerable.

It would appear that my journey has just begun and that my destination is ever changing, but then again, often it is better to travel than to arrive. My question to you would be, are you satisfied with who you are becoming? Make no mistake, it is not an easy or speedy task to go through such a high level of perturbation to bring about change and transformation, but like the caterpillar and the diamond, isn't it worth it? My experience tells me that yes, wholeheartedly, truthfully and without an iota of doubt, it is definitely, definitely worth it.

ABOUT THE AUTHOR: *Pascale Battrick*

Pascale Battrick is a life coach and international from-the-stage trainer known as The Rainmaker, because she precipitates growth and success for all who work with her.

Since 2005 Pascale has been involved in the personal, lifestyle and education development fields and has travelled the world educating herself, researching her craft and teaching hundreds of people from varying cultures and lifestyles, using her unique training style. She's energetic, inspiring and highly motivational as she teaches people to become the empowered transformers they inherently are - the powerful changers of their own lives.

Pascale's first entire book, 365 Days of Sunshine, is due for release in 2014.

Rainmaker Coaching and Training can be found at http://www.PascaleBattrick.com.

Chapter 4

Conscious Creating

By Kaarin Allsa

You are a spark of divine consciousness and regardless of how you label the divine, it resides in you. The power of creation was granted you by virtue of that internal relationship. Every day, whether you are conscious of it or not, the world around you changes in direct response to your deepest needs and desires. So if that is true, why isn't the full realization of your desires your everyday experience?

The answer is simple; it's because you haven't yet learned how to create consciously.

Being a conscious creator isn't so much about learning how to create. You are already a creator. It's more about learning how to create with conscious intent. When your thoughts are clear and you make a conscious request of life, delivery is arranged.

When you remain an unconscious creator, your mind waffles and vacillates. You react to your experience such that the divine in you becomes confused. Your requests of your creative force may even be contradictory. Remaining unconscious of your creative ability means you turn off the belief that you are the creator and your mind turns things inside out, believing instead that you are not the creator at all. Preferring to believe that you are at the mercy of a creative force that resides somewhere far removed from any input you have.

Becoming a conscious creator means you no longer remain reactive to the life you experience. It means you turn 180 degrees and remember that you are the creator of the life you experience.

The good news is that it's simpler than you might think.

Creation Formula

There is a simple formula for creating consciously.

In fact, this formula is so simple that it's easy to regard it as silly or without worth, especially if you've tried manifestation methods in the past with limited effect. Often the limited effect is simply because one of the five essential steps was neglected.

These five steps are essential:

1. Know what you want

2. Clear resistance and fear

3. Manage your thoughts

4. Create a blueprint

5. Ignite the blueprint

Even though the formula is simple, each step can require you to change how you see yourself and your life. But I promise you, with each step you master, the next step gets easier. And by the time you are actively and purposefully igniting your blueprints, you will be manifesting your desires with aplomb.

And it begins with step one; to create what you want, you must know what you want.

Step One: Know What You Want

Over the years, I've found that the majority of people who come to me for help in creating the lives they want, tend to stand on opposing sides of the knowing-what-they-want issue. The first group believes that they know exactly what they want. Yet when we drill into their desires, we find that someone else molded these desires for them. Perhaps they listened to their parents, their spouses, their bosses, or society at-large. And when we strip away the blueprints imposed by the desires and judgments of others, these people usually find that their true desires were dramatically different from what they originally thought.

It's easy to see that putting your creative energy into something that looks like a great treasure to someone else, but has little or no worth to you, creates a high likelihood of failing to produce pleasing results.

The second group of people has no idea what they want. They believe they can't figure it out. As a result, they are confused and often depressed. Generally, they arrived at this confusion by one of three internal processes:

1 Fear of judgment when their desires become known,

2. Resistance to changing in ways necessary to bring their true desires into fruition, or

3. Belief that they are not deserving of, or talented enough to create, their true desires.

All three of these internal processes, left unchecked, will lead a person to any number of mediocre and painful life situations. Often people in this group hide from their disappointment through addiction or unconscious excess.
It's easy to see that hiding from your true desires can't bring them to fruition. Hiding from your desires gives you increasing opportunity to become someone who will never receive what they want.

Regardless of which group you stand in, the truth of

your desires is no further from you than your own heart. The only thing that might stand in your path is self-imposed resistance and fear. To manifest your desire, you must first clear your fear.

Step Two: Clear Resistance and Fear

Once you find your desires, you may also find that a variety of new fears and internal obstacles surface to hinder your ability to take action toward your goals. If you listen to these fears, your body will thrust you headlong into the fight, flight, or freeze response.

You don't have to clear every fear, but you do have to calm your fears enough that they become manageable. The more you can clear, the better. But you don't have to be perfect to be an excellent creator.

You can clear 80 to 90 percent of your fears by consciously accepting that life is going to change as a result of manifesting your true desires. There are no voids in your life right now. It may feel like there are voids, but there are none. I guarantee that your life is full; it's merely a matter of what it is full of!

New things can only come to you if there is a place for them to land. They cannot come into a life that has no room. By accepting that life is going to change, you give tacit permission for those things that do not match your desires to leave. This leaving of old, unwanted things – whether they are tangible items, internal beliefs, or people – creates both the energetic movement of flow and the space for new desired things to enter your life and stay.

To ensure that what comes into the space created by change is actually something you want, you must manage your thoughts.

Step Three: Manage Your Thoughts

Every thought you have is alive with the creative force. Every thought, if sparked, has the opportunity to mold your life. If you want to be a conscious creator, it is essential that you manage your thoughts.

Many people erroneously believe that they must be perfect at this. They mistakenly believe that all thoughts that are not positive must vanish! All thoughts that are judging and fearful must be irradiated!

It's just not so!

You can have as many thoughts of any kind as you like, and if you choose not to give them life, not to give them the energy of attention and belief, they will fall away like so much unwanted debris.

Managing your thoughts is about predominantly highlighting and sparking with belief those thoughts that are in line with the vision of your desire.

Even though all thoughts carry the creative force, only those thoughts sparked with attention, belief, and desire will have enough energy to actually make those desires manifest. So pay attention to the thoughts that you like. Give yourself reason to have thoughts that are in line with who and what you want to manifest and allow the rest to go unattended.

Do not hide any of your thoughts. Merely carefully select the thoughts you wish to spark into life. Use affirmations, read books in line with your desires, talk to people who support these desires. In other words, consciously align with and choose those thoughts that are consistent with the blueprint of your desires.

Step Four: Create a Blueprint to Manifest

A blueprint is a pictorial creation of what you want to create. You can only create what you can imagine is possible. Creating a blueprint of your desire requires being able to see that desire made manifest in your life. The better you are at creating the blueprint, the more likely it will come into fruition. And sometimes the fruition of a desire in your life looks exactly as your blueprint depicts it, and sometimes the fruition of a desire looks a little different but fulfills and even exceeds the desire pictured in the blueprint. The point is that the better you are at imagining it, the more likely it is to happen.

The secret to creating a successful blueprint is giving it as many dimensions as possible. A flat two-dimensional drawing is less powerful than a full-color painting. Something you can only experience with your eyes is less powerful that something you can also touch, taste, and smell.

The more detailed and rooted in sensory experience your blueprint is, the easier it is to ignite.

Step Five: Ignite the Blueprint

You are finally at the last step. You know what you want. You've cleared most of your fear regarding the manifestation of this outcome. You've accepted change and made room for new things to enter your life. You've created thoughts that support your outcome and minimize thoughts that pose resistance. And you can imagine the outcome in vivid detail.

Now it's time to find your passion. If you truly want something, it's easy to find passion to support that desire. And it doesn't matter what kind of passion you use. Many find the passion of joy to be an excellent passion to ignite their blueprint. Others find the passion of love, or peace, or sexual expression. The only thing that matters when igniting the blueprint is finding a passion that lights you up inside with absolute desire such that you can extend that passionate desire to the thing you wish to make manifest.

Below is a short guided-meditation called Igniting the Blueprint that brings these steps together. Do this process once a day until your desire is created or you wish to change the outcome:

1. Get into a comfortable position, close your eyes, and relax.

2. Select a desire you want to create and state to yourself the desired outcome.

3. Begin to imagine this outcome as you want to see it occurring. Pretend that it has already come to pass and see your life as it exists at that moment. Let go of all restraints on your thinking. Tell yourself it's alright to imagine anything, regardless of whether you think it's probable or even possible.

4. Involve as many parts of your brain as you can by giving the imagined outcome multiple dimensions. Hear the sounds present when the outcome is realized. Smell the air, feel the temperature in the environment. Bring in sensations of taste if appropriate to the blueprint you are constructing with your mind.

5. Now, see into the periphery of the picture. What elements of life are around you? Who is with you? Make the colors and elements of your imagined outcome vivid. If people are present, what are they saying to you? What are you saying to them?

6. Now, as you continue to experience the vivid picture you have created, feel the feelings you imagine will overcome you when this outcome is realized. Do you feel joy? Do you feel satisfaction? Do you feel relief from pain or fear? And as you imagine the

feelings you will have, bring them close and begin to actually feel them AS IF the feelings are already present, already realized.

7. Make these desired feelings as strong as you can. If you are happy then laugh aloud! Let the emotions become real.

8. Sustain these desired emotions as long as you can, but no more than a minute.

9. And then let everything go. Let go of the emotions, let go of the picture.

10. You have now ignited the blueprint and given yourself an internal guide toward your desired outcome.

You are now a conscious creator!

ABOUT THE AUTHOR: *Kaarin Alisa*

Kaarin Alisa has honed her abilities in the metaphysical and energetic arts as a spiritual adviser, clinical hypnotherapist, teacher, medical intuitive, and energy practitioner for over forty years. She has helped scores of people realign to their highest truth, so they are free to pursue their dreams and ambitions.

Using her remarkable gifts of penetrating intuition and psychic wisdom along with guided meditations and plain common sense, Kaarin is dedicated to raising consciousness, one person at a time. Her life's work centers on helping people find, and stay true to their paths. Based on information from your aura, body, guides, and higher self, Kaarin can help you heal, grow, and become more conscious as you make progress toward your desires.

She is the creator of Rabika, a card divination and guidance system for the conscious creator. Receive instant, free online-readings and learn more about Rabika at http://www.rabika.com.

Kaarin has also created the Goddess Speak Project to help conscious, entrepreneurial woman bring their messages of change to the world. To learn more about the Goddess Speak Project, go to http://goddess.rabika.com. A sought-after speaker, Kaarin also offers tele-seminars, intensives, spiritual life coaching, and individual energetic sessions by appointment.

Chapter 5

The First Step

By Meesha Salaria

In order to manifest anything, one needs to have a thought, from which is born reality. The Universe gives us more of what we are thankful for. So, it is all about taking the first step and making a START. Manifesting is like magic…all we need to do is to have the courage to take that first STEP and then things follow – believe it!

Why?

Well, "whatever we think about we bring about", we heard that in "The Secret." I must have watched that movie a few times with my Mom and Dad. Maybe that is why I think more about good things in my day than the not-so-good things. That is the reason we should make it a point to appreciate and thank God for all the good things in our lives. I might be a little kid, but I never miss a day and I write in my Joy Journal every day. My Joy Journal has the things I appreciate in my life and that give me Joy.

A good START - a Joy Journal

We should all have a Joy Journal. If we don't have one, we should start one and thank from our heart.

Here's a little story about Lina, the Ballerina. Once upon a time there was a girl called Lina. She was a ballet student who used to criticise everything about ballet. Like "why don't I get the steps, my teacher is so confusing, she isn't doing this properly, and she isn't teaching it properly." One day she told her ballet teacher what she thought. Instead of the ballet teacher getting mad at her, the teacher suggest Lina to start doing a Joy Journal.

The teacher asked her to start a Joyful Journal with positive affirmations in that journal. She asked her to write what she was thankful for, grateful for, and to write what she appreciated in others and in herself. Lina did not like this idea at all, but to please her teacher she decided to START one. To her surprise, Lina started being very happy and positive. She was able to do all the ballet steps, and STARTED liking the instructions her teacher gave. She started loving herself and she made many friends and was very popular. And most of all, she became a stunning ballerina who could do the most complicated steps. She no longer had stage fright anymore. She became the talk of the town. Lina was very pleased with herself. Everyone loved this new Lina very much. She made her parents so proud. She made her teachers and school so proud. Her brother no longer fought with her because she had become an instant hero and she had no time for fights as she would rather practice her ballet or write her

Joy Journal with yummy positive things she's grateful for and would like. After Lina finished school she continued to write the Journal and practise her ballet. Lina, the Ballerina became one of the most famous ballerinas in the world.

I love writing my Joy Journal every day. This Joy Journal will remind me of my beautiful memories when I become older. Because I write it first thing in the morning, I always have a positive start to my day and my daily routine. I also love drawing on the Joy journal while I write as it reflects on how I feel through my drawings. I love writing…just LOVE IT! I guess it gives me the buzzzzzz!

May I suggest that we all start the Joy Journals and experience MAGIC like Lina did. It only takes a few minutes, you know.

We should be grateful for what we have, and not what other people have. Let's love ourselves and our things and love other people. I don't mean to ask to send them a flying kiss or presents. What I mean is to give people energy and ask God to bless them. God has given us a big sack that is filled with love (which is really 'energy'). If we use it all the time, God keeps refilling it. Since we have a never ending supply of LOVE from God, why can we not give out LOVE to ourselves and others.

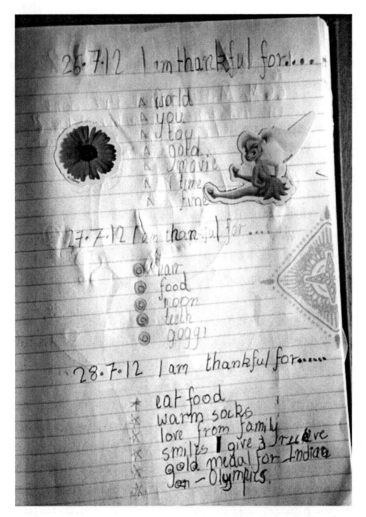

Here's a page from my Joy Journal last year. I never miss a day … and write things I appreciate and Love and am Joyful for.

It STARTS with Determination

Just recently, while we were out and about in our car, I asked my dad if he could put on my favourite song called "The Wild Child" by Enya. Just as he was about to put the song for me, he got a phone call and he didn't get a chance to put on my song. I felt a little upset, but in my heart all I wanted was "The Wild Child", so the only thing I thought about while sitting at the back of the car was I want "The Wild Child". My dad finally got off the phone. We were so hungry that we then started looking for a good café for lunch, but all I wanted was "The Wild Child," not lunch.

After going in circles, we finally found a restaurant but the only thought I had was that of "The Wild Child". Dad asked me to get off the car and walk into the restaurant and when I looked up, to my surprise it said "The Wild Child" so we ended up having a beautiful meal at a restaurant where there were signs everywhere and the signs said "The Wild Child".

This has to be the most amazing experience I had. What I was thinking about was actually happening, but not the way I wanted it. I wanted the song and up were all these signs of "The Wild Child" at the cafe. It sure brought a smile to my face and my mom gave me a cheeky smile to acknowledge what I was already experiencing. But, wait, there is a little more to this story.

To top that up, we went to the library to return the books from the previous week and guess what? The first book I got my glance on (which was in the "Book of the Week" section of the glass cabinet) was a book called the "The Wild Child" by TC Boyle, which is an adult book. I could not believe this was happening to me. How come I got to glance of "The Wild Child" in so many different ways?

This is when it my mom made me realize that it was THE WILD CHILD in me, who wanted the song and I was not specific as to what I wanted though I was so so determined. Mom and I kinda laughed and laughed so much that we had teary eyes. Finally, we sat in the car to come home and my Dad put my song "The Wild Child" by Enya. Yaay! My day was full of The Wild Child.

Guess the Universe does not know the difference between what we have or what we want... what I mean by that is, that I wanted THE WILD CHILD and got THE WILD CHILD in so many different ways (signs at a café and the book at the Library) ...hmmm! Makes you think, eh?

I learnt a beautiful lesson that we should be specific when we want something, because the Universe, I mean our inner Universe makes it happen for us ... Manifests for us, so we might as well be specific!

The question we must ask ourselves, what are we determined to **MANIFEST**? Once we have come up with a few things, we should be **SPECIFIC** about what we want and when we want it, otherwise we will end up with what I did ...ha ha ha.... I got the

"The Wild Child" in different forms and not in the song form – ha ha ha.

I START my shower each morning with Confirmations and Appreciations

The dictionary meaning of con.firm is to establish the truth or correctness of (something previously believed, suspected or feared to be the case).

The dictionary meaning of con•fir•ma•tion is to confirm something, the state of being confirmed.

So, here are the **Confirmations/Appreciations** I do each day. This confirms what I already appreciate, and my Universe gives me more of this to appreciate. I say in a loud voice to trick the trickster mind. So, if the mind fears something or has a doubt, our saying these confirmations aloud tricks the mind to believe that what is being said is the only truth.

This can be done by kids like me or by adults. Positive **confirmations/affirmations** like these made a big difference in me and would you believe it that I have this page laminated and hung on my shower screen, so my sister Aania and I get to say them each day. This was not my idea, I actually saw my parents had their own laminated pages in their bathroom, so I decide to have one in my bathroom. It gives me great pleasure to read them aloud while I have a shower. My sister and I sing it these days.

Have to share a secret with you….Sshhhhh!

One of my **Appreciations/Confirmations** that says I have Beautiful Hair I created when there was a rumour that there had been a case of head lice in the school, I added that one to the list and ever since I say it I have never had head lice. It's been over 1.5 years that we have not had head lice and I am so proud of myself and my Confirmations for this reality.

I LOVE MY LIFE!

Why do I do them each day? My parents call them Affirmations and it is OK, but I call them **Appreciations or Confirmations** because it is to do with appreciation and it confirms to the mind what is said aloud. Saying it every day tricks the trickster mind and the mind starts confirming what I read aloud. Ha ha… found a way to trick the mind.

Would you like to do what I do, but putting the your **Appreciations or Confirmations or Affirmations** at the shower door? Let's start with "I Love Myself and "Everyone is fond of me" and "I am so so so popular".

Magic happens for me when I say these and would love to know what MAGIC that happens when you say yours aloud. Please write to me on meeshabiz@ gmail.com to let me know what your confirmations were and how MAGIC happened for you too.

Miracles come disguised

This is the story of a shy girl named Yasmine, who always found it hard to make friends. Yasmine was eight years old and had just moved to the country due to her father's new job in the countryside. It was her first day at school and she was very nervous and wondered how she would make any friends at this new school. She was really missing her friends from her previous school. When she got to school, she was told that one of the girls got chicken pox and that she was to replace sick girl's position in the Team Relay at the Athletics carnival to represent her school among another 20 schools.

She did not agree at first as it was her first day at school and she was not good at sports. She did not even have her sports uniform or shoes, so the principal organized for her to have all that she needed to represent her school, but she did not agree.

After several minutes when here parents were called to the principal's office and together they all tried to convince her to participate. She finally agreed, but was not so happy about it. No one in the team really spoke to her at first, because she was new and everybody already had friends they hung around with.

She sat with the teacher on the bus to the Inter-School Carnival and was so nervous that she was constantly biting her finger nails and flicking her hair to avoid any eye contact with other kids on the bus, who all had their eyes on her.

They arrived at the athletics arena at the stadium and started lining up to register for the Carnival. Yasmine was mostly standing on her own because of her shy nature and she did not know anyone. How she wished she was not there and instead was at her previous school with all her dear friends. She was a bit teary in her eyes.

Finally, it came the relay race and to everybody's surprise, the shy Yasmine ran like a fine horse. She ran and ran and ran. Because of her, not only did they win the relay race but the school also came second in the Athletics carnival which was fantastic.

Yasmine has to pinch herself to really realize that she was the one who was running in the race. She could not believe herself that she could run the way that she did. She asked herself "What just happened in the race ? Did I really run in the race or was it another Yasmine?" She heard an inner voice saying "Yes, Yasmine…it was you and your team just won the relay."

All kids surrounded her when they got the trophy and gave her hugs and kisses. Teachers were so proud of this new kid at school. They all loved her and on the way back from the Carnival, they all wanted her to sit with them … She was wanted by everyone … everyone wanted to be her friend. At that moment, she said "Thank You, God..

When the school bus arrived back at school, she was greeted with the rest of the team with such honor especially by the principal.

When her mom picked her up from school, she was sur-
rounded by so many friends and teachers and the principal
told her mom what had happened. The mom started crying
to hear that and was very proud to see her daughter so
popular.

She was given an award at the school assembly the following
week for her efforts on her first day at school and she became
a hero. Everyone became Yasmine's friend straightaway.
Not just that, she was on the front page of the newspaper
with a big article on her efforts "New Kid in Town makes
the school proud."

If wasn't for the girl who had chicken pox and was
away, then Yasmine wouldn't have won for her team
and wouldn't have made so many friends on her first
day at school. This had been a **Miracle in Disguise**
for little Yasmine. She made it a vow to take things
as they come from then on because there could be a
miracle waiting around the corner, but it could be
disguised. She said she would see every challenge as
a Miracle in Disguise.

The moral of this story is that **Blessings and Miracles
come disguised**, so we need to recognize that and
take life as it comes because there could be a hidden
Miracle in it. Can you think of a Blessing in Disguise
that ever happened to you? I would love to hear from
you (meeshabiz@gmail.com).

By being grateful for everything (even the challenges)

changes our lives, because the challenges help us learn and help us remember for the next time. It is all about taking the first step even when you know it will be a challenge. Say to God "thank you for this challenge, I know something great is going to come out of it".

I ACCEPT myself for WHO I AM

A little while ago when we moved to the country, I was called "The Dark Kid" at my new school and was teased. This is when I informed the kids at school that I was a 'Yummy Caramel" color.

Either way, the bottom line is that I am dark and no cream or paint can paint me another color. So why bother feeling bad or justifying that I am not. This was the perfect lesson in accepting myself for who I am. I am proud to be born to my Indian parents and am proud of my Indian cultural heritage as well as the Aussie culture.

Some people are dark, some light; some are tall, some short; some have a disability and some are fit as a horse; some have allergies and others don't, some have blue eyes and other brown eyes. At the end of the day, **we are WHO WE ARE**, so how does it matter. At the soul level we are the same and at the physical level we are in different colored bodies.

My parents have always been comfortable with the color of their skin and their heritage. They respect themselves, so they respect others. Somewhere along the line I must have learnt this acceptance from seeing them - **I ACCEPT myself for WHO I AM.**

In life, it is not about judging other people like what they wear what they do. Let's all give love to people we find different, as they may have a story behind it, so let's not make fun of anyone. When we make Life fun for them, Life becomes fun for us. So, I am this "Yummy Caramel Indian" kid, who loves being who I am. I shared this story not to show off, but to share with you that we should all be grateful for who we are and should accept ourselves just how we are. Moral of the story is that "Life is as it is" and nothing can change it, so why not accept it with a smile.

I'd love to share another similar story when I was challenged on stage once. When I was in grade year 1 and was getting an award on stage, I was so excited that I wet myself on stage.

All I could say to myself was "Oh Well…." Did I like what happened to me in front of the whole primary school (teachers, principal, students)? Of course I did not like it. I accepted things for what they were and accepted the prize and award on stage with pride and grace even though several parents had taken a pictures and video of the Award Ceremony and would have captured the moment. I then shared this story in front of the class when it was my turn to do 'show and share'. So many kids felt so comfortable with my story and told me that they had had worse accidents. I felt good that it was a topic of discussion in our class and we made a pact with our class that we should not make fun of the person who has any accident, but to help that person out. I shared this story to share that I accepted myself for who I AM and as a result everyone else did.

One of my favourite teachers, Dr. John F DeMartini once said "No matter what I have done or not done, I am worthy of LOVE" and I live by this each day. I have these words on my bathroom mirror that remind me each day to be worthy of LOVE. Thanks Dr. DeMartini, you are a great teacher and a wonderful friend. I thank you for such beautiful wisdom and for sharing these words with me. My family and I live by these words each day. No matter whatever happens each day at school, I feel I am worthy of LOVE. Because I think I am worthy of LOVE, everyone treats me as though I am worthy of Love.

Though I am a kid, I must tell everyone that we were born in a particular family, in a particular country, in a particular time for a reason. We should all accept 'Life As Is' and contemplate why we are here? What is our purpose ? What can we do for ourselves ? What we can share with others? Why do we want what we don't have ? My friends think sometimes that I am weird, but I love to ask these spiritual questions to myself and contemplate and when I get my answers, I write them in my creative journal which helps me with ideas when I write my next book.

What is Happiness

We all have a gift, and happiness is when we find that gift and share it. Happiness is a celebration with our close friends and family. Not only are we celebrating the successes but also sharing. It could be simple genuine smiles we share, or love we share, or clothes we share or passion we share or food we share or stories we share (like we are doing in this book).

My parents helped me find my gift, which is the gift of writing so here I am sharing these stories with you all. What is your unique gift that you can share with the world ? What is that you have that no one does? What will it take you to share with the rest of us ?

Health

I went vegetarian at the age of five, simply because when I realized that you have to kill an animal, then cook up the dead animal and then eat it; it put me off and I told my mom that I don't want to eat any dead animals.

My parents not only agreed to not forcing me to eat meat, but they also became vegetarians themselves. I am not asking people to become vegetarians just because their kids did, I am just sharing my story. My parents tell me that back in the olden days their moms told them that ALL FOOD WAS ORGANIC as they used to grow most veggies and some fruits at home. That must've been nice.

These days I join in my parents for a water fast where
all we drink is spring water which we collect ourselves
from the natural springs in the mountains. Well, then
we have the juice fast where all we drink is juice...I

only do water and juice fast for a few hours, but it is a lot of fun because when we break the fast we get to have a huge glass of watermelon juice garnished with mint, yum!

We also drink natural spring water that we collect ourselves from a natural spring in the mountains. This water is magical and has special power, especially because we collect it ourselves and fill our Jerry Cans with over 200 litres of natural spring water. This is a fun trip as we take a little picnic with us so while we fill water, we have out little healthy snack picnic too.

 Do you know where your closest natural spring is? You can locate it or http://www.findaspring.com. This is a growing movement, composed of people all over the world, who are choosing to drink the cleanest, healthiest, most natural water…and you can find it anywhere in the world. So, give it a go and donate generously.

Dehydrated Fruits

You know, I take raw food to school as well and though kids at first made fun of my lunchbox that had organic raw mushrooms, zuchini, carrots, avocados, tomatoes, celery, fruits, berries, dehydrated fruits, nuts & seeds. Now I see the same kids bringing some of that food to school. It makes me feel so good when people make the effort to eat good raw foods especially kids my age. A healthy diet, means healthy food, which means more energy for all of us.

Sun is the energy and sun helps the plants grow when we have raw plant-based foods, we get energy in us. It is a good idea to have lots of plant-foods and raw is better because we get Sun's energy that energizes us and makes up happy.

I have one golden rule when doing raw foods. I cook or prepare raw food when I am in a good mood, then eat when in a good mood because when you cook in a bad mood and you eat your food when you cooked in a bad mood it will go in your body and could even make you sick with bad energy. "WE ALL DESERVE TO BE HAPPY," so why not be in a happy mood when we cook and eat !

Yummy Raw Chocolate Mousse

Prepare Ingredients:

- ½ cup Organic Agave or Honey or Maple Syrup
- 1 sliced Organic Avocado
- 1 tbsp Organic vanilla extract (or bean paste)
- ¼ cup Organic Carob powder or Cacao powder
- ¼ cup Organic Coconut Water or Water

- Pinch of Organic Himalayan Salt.
- Pinch Organic Cinnamon
- Unconditional Love

Blend Put all ingredients in a Vitamix or high speed blender in order as listed above for 30 seconds (or until smooth and creamy).

Spoon into bowls with Love and set in the fridge Garnish with Mint, Berries Strawberries & Love. Serve with Love and Smiles ;-)

p.s; My recipe book should be out soon, but for now, if you would like the recipe, feel free to write to me on meeshabiz@gmail.com and I'll email it to you.

Respect for Mother Earth

Health is very important as it shows how much we respect the earth. When we look after ourselves, the earth nurtures us like a mother. When I have a shower, I am in bare feet and get to thank mother Earth for the ability to feel it when showering, so when I have a shower it shows I like to keep the earth clean, if I am messy it shows I litter on the earth. Earth is our home. Earth is our mother. It is what we live on, so today let's go and pick one piece of rubbish to clean our earth. It is where we came from. It is where we live and it is where we go when we leave earth.

Did you know that when we breathe in we get good

energy from the trees and when we breathe out the trees take our bad energy and turn into good energy. If we have a shower and have cleaned the earth then we can manifest better in a clean space. They say if we are clean it shows how clean our mind is. No one thinks in your mind but us, so we can create anything we want. If we were taught that the world is scary place it will be a scary place.

If we think the world is a joyous place we will have a fantastic life as it will be a joyous experience. If each one of us takes up the challenge to do something for mother earth, expecting nothing in return, then MAGIC will happen. Right now let's change the way we think and turn to mother earth and give it love like we would to our own parents.

Lots of Love, Meesha Salaria

ABOUT THE AUTHOR: *Meesha Salaria*

Meesha Salaria is an 8-year-old published author and entrepreneur. Here's a sneak peak of her book START on: http://www.amazon.com/Start-begin-Beginning-Meesha-Salaria/dp/1452552193#reader_1452552193.

Meesha Salaria was seven years old when she published her first book "START: to Begin with Beginning". She is passionate about life. She gets inspired by simple things in life and looks up to great teachers like T. Harv Eker, Blair Singer, Deepak Chopra, Wayne Dyer, John Kehoe, Marjean Holden, Anthony Robbins, Dr Johm F DeMartini and so many more entrepreneurs for inspiration.

It is her desire to share her stories and her thoughts with people, so she could contribute to Planet Earth that Buzzes with inspirational Energy. She is an author who enjoys writing books to share her stories with people, as her contribution to the Planet Earth which is such a Beautiful Place. She loves her school, her teachers and her friends.

"I really love writing, I love sharing, I love to contribute ... just got to work on my typing speed and touch typing. I asked mom to buy me a typing software that can teach me to type really fast so I can write more and more books."

How To Connect With Meesha!

web: http://www.meesha.biz
web: http://www.meeshasalaria.com
facebook: http://www.facebook.com/meeshabiz
FB Fan Page: http://www.facebook.com/meeshabiz

Chapter 6

Changing a Habit is Changing Our Minds

By Janet Janssen

"When I was a teenager I had set 3 goals to accomplish in my life: Go Sailing, Write a Book and ride in a Lear Jet."

In the fourth grade at Los Altos Elementary school in Whittier, California, our class had a huge history project. We were going to make a movie about Pocahontas, John Smith and the Pilgrims, a Thanksgiving Day movie. I was the lead actress. My mother had made an outfit for me with hanging fringes just like the real Indians must have worn, I thought. In one of the scenes, I meet up with John Smith and the Colony of pilgrims behind him. I greeted them with the spoken line "Hau", with the Indian hand gesture. This was my first acting role, and I had a talking part in a movie! I still remember. After watching the late 60s movie "I Want to Live" starring Susan Hayward, I was struck with her character's role, who is accused of murder. She was a tough ol' broad and her personality did not serve her character well. She was given no sympathy. I recall her bravery in taking her last breath before she was gassed to death. What strikes me now was her desire to want something so badly, but in her case she was denied this choice by hard cold justice. She paid the consequences for her behavior.

My point here is about desire. She wanted something so badly and she was not able to accomplish it. It was taken from her. She committed a crime and had to pay the piper. She hung around with savory characters; life was tough and she became tougher. She had good personality characteristics of loyalty and dedication, but these were misplaced and given to the wrong kind of people. She put herself in jeopardy and the unthinkable happened. She wanted to live, but it was too late. She became the victim of circumstances that she had created.

This movie speaks about wanting to change something when it is too late. It tells us a story about a woman who became a victim. Her choices and decisions in life lead her in into harm's way. Her habits were deep-seated, not visible to the naked eye and they were born in her mind first.

In most cases, we are not standing before a jury and begging for our lives. We have the freedom of choice;

although sometimes the internal frustration of changing a habit can feel more painful than the elation of the possibility of freedom. Changing a habit is about making a decision and from this point on is where the real work begins. But, one must recognize that something needs to be changed first.

I would like clarify several points about this chapter. We are not changing good habits; we are changing habits that harm us physically, emotionally and spiritually. I will be talking about how our habits come from our internal thinking patterns, how they were born and how we can change them. Changing a habit is not for sissies. Changing a habit is about taking responsibility for the very person who created the habit in the first place, you.

The 5 Key Concepts

Changing a habit or an addiction for that matter, takes desire, motivation and perseverance, and you must do the work and in many cases get support.

I explore five key concepts that will help you create a plan for change. I will share anecdotes that demonstrate how habits are formed in early childhood, and how these can germinate inside our heads resulting in poor habit choices and behaviors.

Susan Hayward would be proud of me," I thought, while walking through the brush to later greet John and the Pilgrims who arrive at my Tippy. This was quite an elaborate set for fourth graders. Thinking back now, I realize Mrs. Koswalski was quite an amazing teacher. But, I would forget this part about her. When production rapped up and we needed to do voice-overs, my timing was off. It was hard. I just couldn't do it right and the teacher decided to have another female student do the voice-over for me. I was devastated. I had failed in front of my peers.

Let me introduce you to my dad. He was a good provider for our family and still today prides himself for his role as a good family man and deservedly so. He demonstrated the role of responsibility and reliability well, but you would be correct in assuming I had issues with my daddy. I had held onto what becomes known as grudges longer in my life than is healthy. It would be at his 80th birthday party when I was finally able to connect some of the dots about how feelings turn into thoughts, thoughts into beliefs and how they can show up in our lives, negatively.

These connections relate to beliefs that I formed early on and held onto well into my adulthood. I was embarrassed that I couldn't do the voice-over for my Pocahontas role. I was ashamed. These anecdotes exemplify how my beliefs, learned at an early age fueled my negative habits of thinking. How they stifled my dreams and aspirations throughout my life. How I acted on these beliefs and developed patterns that showed up in my relationships and career choices and career changes.

Changing a habit or behavior is entwined in our beliefs systems and only through soul searching and investigation can we sort out the good, the bad and the ugly. These next two anecdotes describe how past events and experiences can sink deep into our unconscious young minds. You must first know that I started kindergarten at age four, so I was a year younger than my peers, but was showing some educational promise.

Pocahontas was beginning to struggle with math, specifically thought problems. My dad was smart, tall at 6'1" and as a young girl I had been infatuated with his handsome good looks, but now he was becoming a figure of authority, stern and disciplined. He showed little patience in teaching me how to do thought problems. I just couldn't understand them. He tried and tried and I cried and cried. He called me stubborn and I felt stupid.

Fourth grade also offered a huge opportunity for me and a major family disaster occurred. The teacher had talked with my parents about me skipping fifth grade. Apparently the thought problem issue was not such a big deal with the teacher or school system. I recall being good at spelling, art, history, science, and considered very creative. But my parents decided against the upgrade. They felt I was too young and perhaps would have issues with me being so young as a sixth grader. I believe they made this decision thoughtfully, but back then I felt differently. I do recall trying to change their minds, but they didn't believe in me. "I was not worthy or smart enough," I thought.

I had two younger sisters, Mary Lou, and Carmen, who was just a baby. Mary Lou was three years younger than me, Carmen three years her junior. Mary Lou died on the operating table from a failed heart surgery operation at age four and half. She was born with a hole in her heart, called a 'Blue Baby.' Back in the 1950s, they sewed patches over the hole and the technology was crude compared to today. It was devastating for my parents. I was angry. And what made this true story sadder was how my sister and I integrated this loss.

Both Carmen and I had many discussions about this situation as we grew older. Both my parents did the best that they could do, but the messages you hear as children often become your truth, not what your parents or role models necessarily say. According to behavioral psychology, our core beliefs are sealed inside our impressionable minds between the ages of three and seven years old. Mary Lou became the poster child in our family. She died and her memory lived on, and we felt left behind.

I believe we can all understand that losing a child is a heartbreaking experience for parents and siblings. I hated God for taking her and resented Mary Lou for getting so much attention in my life after she was gone. The real kicker for Carmen and I was coming to terms with a comment my mom often spoke: "Mary Lou was so pretty." Carmen and I developed a sense of humor about this statement. We had to.

We would snipe together with acerbity, "She was the pretty one and we were chopped liver!" Mary Lou stayed young, sweet and beautiful our whole growing up years and we knew we could not compete for our mother's love because of this. The loss of a loved one can be very cruel for the living and developing healthy models of coping skills is often missed in the family unit. Professional help would have been helpful for me, but it never happened.

So, before I am eight years old, I formed some rather unhealthy beliefs about myself. I am not good at anything, I am stubborn, I am not pretty, my parents don't believe in me and I am stupid. Sad, right? What is especially sad is that this is not what my parents were telling me specifically or intentionally. I will not defend the fact that perhaps they might have been more aware of my delicate psyche, but it is clear to me now that they were not trying to be cruel and did their best at the time. This realization took intention.

I believe changing a habit is changing our minds. This chicken and egg title was intended. How we change any habit or behavior or thought pattern does take intention and we must be awake to this reality. Most importantly, change is not for people who need it, but for people who want it. Recognition and intention are the precursors to change, and getting into action is implicit.

In other words, if you want different results some-thing must change.

At 60 years old, I was asked to organize my Dad's 80th birthday party, outside of Las Vegas. My husband and I live in the Santa Cruz Mountains in California, about 11 hours from Las Vegas, Nevada. At the birthday party, I overheard my dad speaking to group of his friends at one of the tables. He was talking about me and a discussion he had had with one of my teachers. I had organized this whole birthday event for my dad. At the event, I was getting compliments from our family and his local friends for making his birthday so special. I had written lyrics to a song and sang it telling stories about my dad's life. Yes, ever the actress and admittedly, the song was clever and fun.

Nonetheless, he was telling his friends about the discussion he had had with one of my teachers. She had told him that sometimes the qualities of stubborn-ness can show up later in life as positive, so to give me a little time. He was laughing while telling his friends about how stubborn I was as a child. I cringed inside recalling the internal frustration at sitting at our dining room table feeling hopeless and stupid, because I didn't understand the thought problems. Dad was irritated and impatient with me. I remember feeling hopeless, incompetent and eventually had to give up, a common pattern of thinking in my career life.

I realized at my dad's 80th birthday party how I was still yearning for his approval. Instead of telling a story to his friends about what an awesome daughter I was for organizing and putting this whole event together for him, he was telling them about how he had to be patient and watch my stubbornness mature into something better. I guess it was a back-handed compliment, but at the time I was pissed. I was 60 years old and still struggling with daddy issues.

Recognition

However, I was able to let go of my past hurt and disappointment, but not right away. I had made a conscious decision after that weekend to do so. I set about having a plan in doing more work. The work is about introspection, personal assessment and deciding that personal change can happen. I knew I could do this.

That weekend at my dad's event, my poor husband had to listen to me complain about my dad not appreciating me. I was wounded and hurt and knew at the same time, the inventory was mine.   A part of being an adult is self-nurturing. We must make the decision to change. We must take the bull by the horn, not someone else. So now at 60, I realized I had more work to do. I knew this, because at age 36, I had let go of other self-destructive habits and behaviors, many addictive in nature.

In this chapter, I will not be going into any great depth about my past dysfunctional behaviors and habits, but enough to tell you that I qualify to talk to you about change. The fact, that I let go of alcohol, drugs, cigarettes and various other co-dependent behaviors, qualifies me to talk about changing habits, recovering from addictions and how they formed and more importantly how you can change. It takes courage. It takes willingness to do the work; again and again. No change, no change.

How then did my low self-worth and esteem impact my life? What kind of habits and behaviors were formed? How did I overcome them and why do I say that changing a habit is changing our minds? In my upcoming book, "21/30 Club: Change a habit and Create New Brain Power for Success," I will be addressing these answers in more depth, but for now I would like to introduce you the general concepts about habit change.

Changing a habit does take making a decision and the belief that we can. Have you ever noticed how some habits keep repeating themselves? Little habits or big ones, we try, we give up and we try again? We know this is not uncommon behavior among humans, because we tend to seek pleasure over the perceived pain of change.

In the field of neuroscience, we are introduced to the fact that with every thought an electrical impulse is fired off from a neuron. This electrical pulse shoots over to another neuron creating a pathway and with each repetitive firing and repeated redundant behavior or thought this pathway becomes stronger and stronger. In fact, this pathway becomes so strong that we can become unconscious and repeat patterns like driving a car, grabbing for the milk container to pour over our cereal and repeated patterns of thinking happen almost naturally. The unconscious mind takes over.

I have been on diets, where unless I kept a diary, I would easily forget I ate snacks in-between the meals. I would forget how many cigarettes I had smoked until the pack was almost empty. And, I have said things to myself, like 'that was stupid' over and over again without even being consciously aware that this negative statement had been said.

And it is important to note here, the brain believes whatever I say — positive or negative.

Neuroscience has become mainstream, bursting with information about how the brain operates and how it influences behavior and vice versa, another reason I chose my chapter title. We go to the gym to work out and tone our muscles, build flexibility, strength and stamina. We know working out the brain makes the brain healthier, increases flexibility, neuroplasticity, prevents aging, diseases and becomes the positive influencer of making healthy habit changes stick!

The old joke, "my thinking is a like a bad neighborhood, don't go there," holds some truth behind it. From biblical scripture to modern day inspirational gurus, 'What a man thinketh he becomes," is now backed up by neuroscience studies. What we think matters.

In my pilot program for the 21/30 Club, I built into the program a way to track a negative habit, change it, and reframe it in 21 days. The process of changing a negative habit into a positive one and creating a new neural pathway in support of this is possible in 30 days. What fun to combine both efforts into one program.

This program is not held in any scientific laboratory, provides no SPECT or MRI scans, but instead is based on a simple premise. If you are willing to follow a daily program for 30 days using sound basic principles, and by using basic concepts of behavioral management to feed your brain positive affirmations and actions over and over again, this will jump start your thinking and reinforce a new habit.

The basic five key concepts are really simple too, and little did I realize how I had been using them. Organic in nature these concepts are designed to allow you to flow from one concept to another. Linear 'to do' lists and instructions are often rigid in nature. If you miss one, then what? The recovery process itself is often three steps forward and two steps back. Using these concepts in a cyclical way, you can move forward then back again if needed. This too appeals to both left-right brain preferences. It works, but you must do the work.

Beliefs

So then, how did my erroneous beliefs show up in my life, learned so early in life? Feeling stupid showed up everywhere. In high school, I started cheating on tests. I allowed my conscience to be OK with being dishonest. Years later, I would joke to friends that if I had not cheated in English perhaps writing articles would be easier for me now, and I did come to terms with dishonesty. College was hard too. I was failing in my first semester and had to quit. I told a lie to my college professor that my D grade was because I was working three jobs. I will never forget her response. "Then you should quit one of them." I was stunned. I didn't understand what she was telling me until years later.

Cynthia's Story

Cynthia joined the 21/30 Club for help with an aversion to organizing her office. Recouping from a serious automobile accident, she was also adjusting to a recent move from the home she had grown up in as a child, into a smaller downsized rental with her husband. Anyone might justify this aversion; after all, moving from one place to another is stressful, not to mention her serious accident. She had double whammy of excuses to rely upon.

She wanted a clean and uncluttered office. First, we had to shift through her reasoning as to what was the real issue. Was this aversion related to her recent changes or was there a habit pattern to be recognized, that had a repetitive pattern to it? It became clear through our process that she did not want to use the accident or move as excuses. She recognized the patterns of repeated behavior throughout her life. She recalled, "I wasn't allowed to make my own choices growing up because my father told me that any choice I made was wrong. He would tell me, "I wouldn't like it, finish it or it was too expensive." She grew up not trusting herself to make correct decisions. She proved it to herself over and over again in wrong relationships and staying in jobs and relationships too long. So, behind her aversion was procrastination. The old internal tape was the thought that "It probably didn't matter if I started the job at all, because I would probably never finish it and the off chance I did, it would be wrong anyway," she recalled.

When she looked into her office she had too many choices and possibilities to consider. She became flooded and her internal tapes reinforced her beliefs that to make a decision was complicated and why bother.

She was determined not to let her physical disabilities limit her, and we decided she could proceed with a plan of action, provided that she 'chunk down' the tasks into bite sized actions. Procrastination was the habit. Understanding her old beliefs and their origination around the desired habit change increased her level of motivation and with the support of the group, a simple and realistic plan suddenly became possible. Says Cynthia, "With the 21/30 Club, I was able to make a decision, every day, to do one thing, the same thing over and over, but only for one day at a time. I was able to find an affirmation that was workable and believable for me. I was able to follow through and realize that I had the power to change my life regardless of what I had been taught early on."

Mary's Story

Mary expresses how self-awareness and poor self-worth relates to how she initiated poor habits based on old beliefs and how those beliefs carry into adult lives. She says, "My habit was being addicted to sugar. When I am scared or hurt, I don't want to share these feelings with anyone, so I hunker down and stuff myself with sugar treats to escape these feelings. As a child, I recall Mom and Dad worked a lot and I was home alone often. I recall feeling like there was no one around to hug me and let me know I was okay. The same thing happened if I was afraid. I learned to just dust myself off and move on, so these feelings had just been stuffed down."

"What I learned", said Mary "...and I am not sure where or when I became aware of this fact, but as a scared little girl, I had no one to protect me from the big scary world out there." Sugar became her friend. She is not alone. "When I first started the 21/30 Club with Janet, I was really excited but there was work to be done. I resisted, because at first I got excited about being involved (with a group), but when I had to do homework, I balked." As an adult, Mary was able to recognize her ability to follow through with her commitments, and recognizing this pattern was positive and valuable information for her to know. She said, "I knew I wanted to be a part of the team and not drop out. My "ah ha" moment came when I made the decision to be a part of the team instead of failing at one more thing in my life. I knew I was capable of keeping my commitments. I was on a team with like-minded folks and I knew I did not want to drop out." She recognized that being alone was associated with acting on a behavior that comforted her, but her adult self was capable of making a better choice. Her motivation increased, she had a plan of action and a support system. She recognized she didn't have to fail and believed in her ability to change.

Like these women, I had my own erroneous patterns of behaviors repeated many times in my career lifetime. I would show promise and when things got hard, I had to quit. My resume looks like a rap sheet. I remember in my 20s when one interviewer told me, "You have done so many jobs", I was insulted. I didn't recognize this pattern, until 20 years later. I was completely unconscious about how my negative beliefs about myself were running my careers, relationships; my decision-making choices.

Unworthiness showed up in my first marriage. Instead of dealing with my feelings, I used drugs, because back then everyone was 'doing it' and experimenting; only I got hooked. Later, in future romances, I settled for the frogs, primarily, the emotional unavailable types. I took on the responsibility of showing them how committed and loyal I was. They needed distance and I needed acceptance. Needy is the optimum word. I was unworthy of telling them what I really wanted.

Finally, when I met my husband in 2000, I had figured it out this way. "I want to fall in love, get married and I don't know if you are the one or not, but this is the direction I am heading". I no longer took it personally if some guy was not heading in the direction I was going. I had the attitude of, 'next'. I no longer thought, "What is wrong with me". By the time, the book 'He's Just Not Into You" hit the stands, I understood the dynamic completely.

What I have been talking about is really about emotional intelligence. Having mastery of what we think and feel and how we react to our emotions is key. It is safe to say then: behind every habit is a belief. We have a feeling and we think a thought or vice versa. We must determine quickly where is the thought coming from. Is this the truth or a story we are telling ourselves.

Please know too, this chapter will not be about habits and beliefs entangled with traumatic incidences, emotional or physical abuses. I am not a licensed therapist, so, depending on the core beliefs, getting the right support is encouraged.

I am talking about changing a negative habit. I am talking about changing our negative mind thoughts. Back to the chicken or the egg syndrome.

Motivation

In the 21/30 Club, we address a habit we want to change. We determine what the goal will be, and develop personalized affirmation statements that will be repeated over and over again throughout the course of the program. We journal our thoughts, and take action steps daily. Throughout the program we are tracking our motivational levels.

Often, I hear people say they want to get motivated first in order to change a habit. True, if you are not motivated, change can be very challenging. But, the five key concepts are cyclical, exploring what motivates us and how we chunk down the goal, usually helping us find the belief behind the lack of motivation.

Important too, is to recognize the balance needed for healthy and mental well-being when approaching a habit change. In recovery programs, they talk about the H.A.L.T. theory. When you are too hungry, angry, lonely or tired, this will impact the level of motivation when working with recovery issues. If we are approaching a habit change, I think it is important to recognize how these factors might impact our best intentions.

Recognition, motivation, beliefs, support and having a plan are the key concepts in creating change. Sustainability comes with developing a solid foundation first that will support the daily, weekly processes needed for change. This entire program is about uncovering, discovering and discarding the old, useless thinking patterns and behaviors and replacing them with positive thoughts and behaviors.

The Plan

How to approach changing a habit or behavior requires recognition of the real issue. What beliefs are behind the desire to change and why haven't we been able to change sooner must become a form of introspection. It does take motivation to get the kind of support you need to help you keep moving towards this effort. Why do we want to change and for whom must be clear. Does our desire to change match our motivation and are we willing to do the work? If you are so depressed that you cannot take the action needed to help yourself, as suggested earlier, consider professional therapy.

Failure is not a dirty word. Talk with any successful person you know, anyone who has achieved some hallmark in their life and they will gladly tell you how many failures it took to succeed. I have learned there is a training technique that requires your muscles to fail so that they can be building up strength. Break them down and build them up, so that they become stronger.

We set goals, and have plans so that we can head towards the desired direction. Having a plan does not mean we will met the outcome on time or in a straight projectile. Having a plan provides us valuable information as we move along the pathway, so that we can make adjustments, if needed along the way. I used to want to be the CEO first before paying my dues.

I took guitar lessons because I also wanted to play. After some weeks of practicing, it occurred to me, it takes discipline to learn how to sing and play the guitar at the same time plus coordination. I took singing lessons, to learn I could sing, but my voice is more suited to chorus groups than a hit label at the Grammy Awards. When I auditioned for an acting part in a play and they passed out the schedule for the next six weeks of rehearsals, I balked at the time it would take away from friends and family.

I wanted to write my book in one sitting and thus it never happened. My writer friend Helen said, "Writing is rewriting", so that when I heard her words I was willing to pay the price of good 'ol commitment and dedication. Changing my perspective about what is required of me to succeed at any endeavor is not straight up. It is about taking one step at a time. Having a plan keeps us focused and moving towards what we say we want.

You are reading the words of a woman who has been to hell and back on so many levels. So the movie, "I Want to Live" has a whole new meaning for me and hopefully you too.

My Journey into Action

In the late 1980s, I have a picture of me in a sail boat, steering the rudder. I was drunk at the time, but one goal down. Years later, I sailed in the harbor of San Pedro, in a 19-foot Olympic tempest hanging in the harness in an A Class race. What a blast this was! And, achieving other goals are still on the horizon.

I am now working on goal number two: writing this chapter and the 21/30 Club book. I cannot tell you how many first attempts at 'writing my book' have been made, to only give up. Why? You know the answer. But this time, my dream is being actualized. At this writing, this year, I had four articles published in our local paper, The Banner, as a guest columnist. After the third article was published, my husband said, "Well, I guess you can't say you can't write any more". I have written and posted monthly blogs on my website. My level of self-worth and self-esteem is unbelievable now and here is what I did to get to this point.

Never give up on yourself. I love Churchill's famous quote" Never, never, ever give up".

In giving up my addictions, I did get help. I could not do it alone. I had to come to place of humility, so that my ego took the back seat. I did seek out group support. The power of "we" is greater than "I". I also, turned to spiritual principles of living. Hanging out with the wrong people, like Susan Hayward's character in "I Want to Live" summed it up for me. I was not willing to pay the consequences any further. I quit.

I have adapted principles of living. I use Christian principles, Eastern principles, principles that talk about honesty, open-mindedness and willingness. This is why hanging with healthy like-minded people is so important. I was stealing the minutes of my life away on habits and behaviors that sucked away at the spirit of inspiration, curiosity and meaningful experiences and relationships.

My work as a coach and trainer with Creative Workshops for a Change is about helping people achieve their potential into actualizing them; provided they do they work. As a speaker, I enjoy inspiring others so that they can act, sing, write or change a habit; turning aspirations into a reality! For many years, people told me I had potential. I realized later that what they were saying to me was that I had potential, but I was missing the mark.

Summing It Up

In recovery, from addictions, negative habits or behavior patterns, it is important to recognize what is working in your life and what is not. You have to get brutally honest about who is the common denominator with your negative habits or behaviors to begin with. What is the problem? Better to ask, who is the problem? You are the common denominator and it is You who must face the fact that changing a habit is an inside job.

What we think over and over again determines the outcome of who we become.

Study biographies of famous people. Great leaders find ways to overcome their obstacles. There is no magic to changing our character flaws. We must be courageous and bold and work at changing them. Building the muscles of self-worth and self-esteem take us beyond the great unknown and we become adventurers, explorers and role models for everyone. If you want different results, change the course!

Says Cynthia: "I have a new method of establishing positive habits that I can use on any pattern that I want to change, thanks to the 21/30 Club." Says Mary: "Janet's teaching this program has been so beneficial to me. She has given me so many tools like breathing techniques, mantra's to use, daily quotes and building a vision. Thank you Janet."

Changing a habit is about changing our minds. When your desire to achieve becomes stronger than your desire to give up, you have succeeded at retraining mind thought. The successes in my life from this day forward will always be about believing in me and the willingness in doing the work. We must use common sense and make sure we are supported by positive and loving family and friends. We must take care of our bodies and seek out spiritual reflection and guidance as much as we can handle.

Another amazing benefit to positive habit change is the impact it has on other people.

Lisa's Story

Lisa, another professional business women and member, found surprising results from her habit change. "I had wanted to drink 80 ounces of water daily, but could never get myself to follow through on my own. I was able to recognize what the benefits to me might be by having better hydration in my body, but I did not recognize how I would inspire others to do the same thing. I did not recognize how a positive behavior for me would also help others. This was very inspirational for me." Yes, we can become the positive examples of living for others to follow.

In my work, I am not seeking perfection, stardom or millions of dollars. I am seeking peace of mind that I am following through with my words. Here is my agreement. I will do the work and the Big Kahuna up above will decide the outcomes. It is about the journey and not the destination. And, I haven't forgotten about my Lear Jet ride!

In all of my workshops, I like to tell all my attendee's this one thing, "You are Amazing!"

Be well.

ABOUT THE AUTHOR: *Janet Janssen*

Janet Janssen is a Coach, Trainer, Speaker; Certified Practitioner Hypnotherapy (CHT), Emotional Freedom Therapy (EFT), and Neuro Linguistic Practitioner (NLP). Janet is a dedicated public servant, community educator and creative talent whose mission is to assist individuals, organizations and communities to achieve their desired goals. Her long-term career in business and public relations has given her a fiscally and psychologically sound foundation for her highly professional interventions. She maintains this "results-oriented" approach in her work as an educator. What she has learned from more than 20 years of experience in this field is that there are often internal obstacles in our way that keep us from attaining our personal and professional goals. Those obstacles can sometimes be caused by our own attitudes about ourselves that cause us to remain in stagnant personal or professional situations which don't serve us. Coming from a background of family tragedy and personal difficulties didn't stop Janet from becoming a force for positive change.

Janet's own transformative journey and triumph over painful personal circumstance has made her work with others all the more effective. In guiding others toward fulfillment of their goals, Janet's own passion for a life well lived is renewed. Her mission is to help inspire desire, unleash creativity and topple the obstacles that hold people back from achieving their greatest human potential.

With her sparkling wit and intelligence, and the enthusiasm and energy of a woman half her age, she can elicit laughter and tears through telling relevant pieces of her history, while keeping the group motivated to do their own work.

Janet has a remarkable ability to find fun in any situation, and the participants in her groups and workshops have consistently praised both her work and her demeanor. Drawing upon her own professional and personal experiences, Janet is able to connect with anyone. She encourages balance and reminds us to be grateful for what we do have, and what we have already accomplished.

A dynamic and inventive teacher, she believes that by changing our perspective, facing our fears and disappointments and making the decision to change our self-destructive habits, that we can effect lasting change in our lives that awakens our creative potential and ensures a healthier and more successful future. Having seen this in action so many times during her work with businesses and community groups, Janet is able to offer an array of educational, playful workshops to those interested in this evolution.

Visit her website: www.creativeworkshopsforachange. Sign up for upcoming webinars, audio programs and workshops, available to participants nationwide. She is available for speaking engagements, and is pursuing more online formats.

She is Certified Practitioner of Hypnotherapy (CHT) since 1994, Emotional Freedom Therapy (EFT) and Neurolinguistic Programmer (NLP), Practitioner at Balance Health of Ben Lomond, Felton and Board member: Women in Addiction Association of Treatment Santa Clara (WAAT), Net Worth Recovery Treatment in San Jose, Women's Network Alliance (WNA) of Santa Cruz and President of the Virtual Chapter of WNA and Women in Business Committee of the Santa Cruz Chamber of Commerce (WIB).

Please feel free to contact:
janetjanssen@creativeworkshopsforachange.com

Chapter 7

Learning from Adversity and Failure

By Ralph Cortes

"Defeat is never the same as failure until it is accepted as such."
— Emerson

Fail and fail fast. This is not what we are typically taught in school and our society. However, this is the rule of thumb that most successful entrepreneurs live by. Failure is responsible for stronger and smarter entrepreneurs. What if every defeat was exactly what we needed to push us over the top? What if we welcomed defeat for exactly what it is…a chance to learn, an opportunity to expand. While the circumstances of life are such that everyone must undergo a certain amount of defeat, you can find hope in the knowledge that every such defeat carries with it the seed of equivalent or a greater benefit. Sometimes defeat can be so devastating that men no longer want to try for they no longer see the value in experiencing the sting of defeat. What they failed to do was to use defeat or adversity for what it is a tool, to gauge your success. Yes, defeat and failure are essential parts of your success. Failure and defeat humble so that they may acquire wisdom and understanding. Anyone who has achieved any kind of success is sure to have experience their fair share of failure.

Decide to be grateful for everything that happens not to you, but rather for you. That's right, life is happening for you not to you. You have the incredible power to choose how you feel everyday and to design your life. Even that woefully painful failure is your best friend who is here to serve you, if you choose to accept the lesson each failure holds.

My name is Ralph Cortes, I am truly grateful for the time that you are taking to read this chapter. I am elated that I get a chance to share my story and experience at overcoming failure. My intention for writing this chapter is to be a beacon of hope through the fog of failure and adversity. Do not allow failure to destroy you. Use failure rather to rebuild yourself into a stronger person and transform your character, crystallize your dream, and transfix your determination to succeed through the power of persistence and the fortitude faith. This is your greatest hour -- now learn, live and succeed.

My story begins in the south side of Chicago, in a neighborhood named South Chicago or as it is known South Chi-Ghetto. I am the fourth of six children also known as the black sheep of the family because my way of thinking and actions are different from my siblings. We were from a low-income home, always on a budget and never able to afford the finer clothes and shoes like Nike shoes or Air Jordans. However, my mother instilled in me that if I wanted those things then I would have to work for them. She would give me half the money and I would have to earn the other half. At an early age I learned how to make money and this carried over into my adulthood as I started several businesses and was always able to make money without a problem.

My parents were divorced by the time I was 12 years old, besides that I never seen much of my dad. He was an alcoholic and drug user, so he was in and out of our life. After many attempts my father would later sober up and place a high value on family relationships and served as an inspiration for many. I was abused as a youth growing up, because this is how my mother learned to parent from her parents. At age 15, I joined a gang and ran away from home.

I soon found out that being on my own was not all that it is cracked up to be, having to find a place to sleep as well as something to eat on a daily basis. As I would wake up early in the morning I would have to take care of those two needs first, and then I would proceed to look for ways to party and hang with friends. However, there were times that I was unable to find a place to sleep, so I went to a nearby forest preserve to seek shelter.

I located a little mound in which I proceeded to dig a burrow so that I could crawl into and be somewhat warm, protected from the wind or rain. Some nights I would lie with half my body hanging out the burrow, looking up at the stars and dreaming about being a successful business man with a beautiful home, nice cars and a great income. Living on the street, I soon became accustomed to committing crimes like burglary, strong armed robbery, stealing cars and selling drugs. Survival was key and I was a survivor. I actually enjoyed to freedom of being able to do what I wanted.

Eventually my lifestyle caught up with me and I ended up in Cook County Juvenile Detention Center. Now, the very freedom which I cherished was stripped from me and I was now restricted to my jail cell and the deck, where everyone congregated to play cards or watch TV. Eventually, I beat my case. However my problems were not over just yet. My mother refused to take me home. She told the judge that I was an out-of-control youth. I was this. If I would have stayed on the streets, I was sure to end up dead or in prison. The world I knew was soon turned upside down, as I was now a ward of the state. I was shuffled around from foster home to foster home eventually ending up at Maryville Academy. Maryville was a foster group home for abused and neglected youth. It was here that I learned to set goals and how to prosper while following the rules. I attribute much of my success to learning this skill of goal-setting. I also learned what it is to be far away from home amongst unfamiliar faces, quickly learning how to make new friends. I excelled in every way at Maryville, academically, socially, emotionally. At 17, I joined the Jane Adams Hull House independent living program and now had my own apartment that was paid for by the state until age 21. However I still had the street mentality and I turned back to street ways. I was now selling drugs out of my apartment and living recklessly.

The police were soon watching my apartment. I had people breaking into my apartment to steal drugs, and felt I had to retaliate when I discovered who had broken into my apartment. At 18 years old, I grew tired of this way of being and I knew I would eventually be in prison if I continued the drug dealer lifestyle. Something had to change, either me or my environment. I contacted my DCFS caseworker and told him I wanted to go to college. He said I should enroll at the local community college. By doing this I could still remain in the program and have my school paid for. This was not going to work, I needed to change my environment and get as far away from Chicago as I could. I want to go away to college, to Southern Illinois University. My case worker told me it's not a good idea because I would have to dis-enroll from the independent living program. And if college didn't work out for me I would just end up homeless because I was now an adult. Knowing this, I knew that failure was not an option for me. I believed in myself and took the chance at being the first person in my family to graduate from college.

In my junior year of college, my grades were not that good, and if I had any hope of becoming an attorney, my goal at the time, I would need better grades. What was missing? Why was I failing? It was because I didn't have the discipline needed to succeed in college. So I went to the place which is known for their discipline: The United States Marine Corps.

At first, I was rejected from the corps two times, but I was determined to become a Marine so I would go through three recruiters until my brother Joel hooked me up with his recruiter, who pushed me through. Life in the Marine Corps was great; I loved it and was meritoriously promoted several times. I left the Corps to finish my schooling and found myself unemployed for a whole year. Interview after interview, rejection after rejection I proceeded to keep on trying because I couldn't give up. Failure was not an option.

Luckily my Marine Boxing team Coach Staff Sergeant Hermin Isidro, who was better known as Coach, talked me into getting my Commercial Driver's License to drive semi trucks, just in case things didn't work out like I planned. It is with a great sense of gratitude that

I am glad I listened to him. It was now time to use my CDL even though it had been years since I drove a truck. As I applied at various trucking companies, they told me that I needed to take a $300 refresher course because it had been to long since I last drove. I proceeded to ask family for the $300, unfortunately everyone was financially strapped and they said no. However a good friend I helped out years earlier would borrow me the $300.

As a truck driver, I soon bought my own truck and started my own company within eight months. In the years to follow I would successfully turn that $300 seed into over $1 million, trucking was good to me. I would go on to buy more equipment and eventually my first apartment building. Trucking provided me the means to be able to make these life changing purchases and helped me to build wealth.

It was now time to give back to Maryville. As a successful businessman I returned to Maryville academy. This was a goal I had set the very day I left Maryville at 17 years old. I was now teaching the children at Maryville about success, and much of the personal development material I had learned through the years. I was able to mentor these kids because of the adversity and failure that I had experienced. Being able to guide them with the hard-earned wisdom that I acquired from my mistakes, I could make a difference in their lives. I showed them how to use the adversity they were experiencing by being in a foster group home to propel them towards success. This is my story of overcoming adversity and failure by believing I could be more then I was. Believing that I could achieve success in whatever area I chose. Failure was not an option for me, I encourage you to take on this same mindset and watch your beautiful life full of success and prosperity unfolds before your very eyes. I have learned several techniques and tools to overcome my failures and adversity, which I will now share with you.

Turning Obstacles into Opportunity

"One who gains strength by overcoming obstacles possesses the only strength which can overcome adversity." — Albert Schweitzer

Each obstacle is a chance to expand and grow as a person develops character. Can I really turn obstacles into opportunities? You might ask yourself, and I am here to reassure you that you can. Imagine that every obstacle an opportunity for advancement or a chance to gain wisdom. It's an entirely different point of view and a very helpful one at that. This in fact is the same process that many entrepreneurs use to find out what their next endeavor will be. They search for a problem that an industry or person is having, then attempt to solve that problem, bringing value to that person and being compensated for their problem-solving skills. One of the benefits of failure is that you can learn from it.

The benefits of failure are numerous and wonderful when they are utilized. In my life I have met several people who have turned their situation around because they changed their point of view. As simple as this may seem this is the key to changing many things, many people fail to keep a positive mental attitude when it comes to these things. This can make all the difference as you will see as in this chapter. Wisdom is the variable that will elevate you to the next level when it is cultivated properly in the right way. Life can be so different when you look at it from a different perspective.

A great illustration of turning obstacles into opportunity is the life of Charles Hew-Len, who I had the pleasure of meeting through a friend. Charles is from Waianae, Hawaii which is one of the roughest towns in Hawaii. Tourists are warned not to venture to that town, because of the violence, drugs and criminal element. The schools in Waianae were ranked last in the whole state of Hawaii. Charles admits that he was not a brain in school, he was actually ranked in the lower percentile of his class.

As a casualty of a poorly-run school system, Charles never learned to read. Instead he did what most kids from his housing projects did to make a living: he sold Meth. That choice cost him dearly and when he was caught he got eight years in prison, then his wife divorced him and took his kids. His world was turned upside down and he was at the bottom. While he was in prison he learned to read.

The first book that he read was *Awaken the Giant Within* by Anthony Robbins, which introduced him to the world of self development. Another benefit of being in a minimum security prison was he was housed with white collar criminals, businessmen that made some wrong choices. He befriended these men and soon was being taught about business and real estate. Charles was released from prison and began to practice what he was taught. Although it was challenging, living in a halfway house, unable to travel except for work, no cell phone, running his business from a payphone with a handful of quarters, he was persistent and driven to succeed no matter what obstacles faced him.

He soon had his first real estate deal done, several deals soon followed. Upon release from prison, Charles had set a goal, to have $100,000 in his bank account in one year. Charles reached that goal and would surpass it by a whole lot. Two years after being released from prison, he was now a millionaire because of his real estate success. He now gives his time and money to better his community and is a model citizen and businessman. He was recently voted as one of Top 20 emerging leaders by Hawaii Business Magazine. Prison, halfway house, financially broke, no office, born into poverty, these were the obstacles that Charles faced and he turned each of those into opportunities that would shape the phenomenal business man he is.

How to Learn from Failure

"Its fine to celebrate success but it is more important to heed to lessons of failure" — Bill Gates

Each Failure or Defeat is the opportunity to learn, and if you adapt this mindset then each and every time you experience failure or defeat you be the able the harness the insightful power that can only be experienced by failure and defeat. You might ask, "How do I learn from failure?"

Here are a few simple steps on how to learn from failure.

1. Take the risk and pay the price. Don't be scared and let fear keep you from learning the valuable lesson that failure may have in store for you.

2. Know it's OK to fail, really. Be comfortable with the possibility that you might fail, be ready to learn.

3. Realize that experience is the best teacher.

4. Allow yourself the freedom to fail.

5. Let the fear of failure help you to succeed.

6. Welcome failure…if you're not failing then you're not growing.

Questions to Ask to Overcome Failure

Another great tool to overcome or make failure relin-
quish its pearls of knowledge is questions. The better
the quality of the question, the more useful the answer
will be. The answer will assist you in learning from
failure. I remember hearing Anthony Robbins state
that the quality of your life is directly related to the
quality of questions you ask yourself. It is essential
to demand the most out of failure by presenting it
with quality questions. A few examples of question
to assist you are:

1. What is failure? What is success? Who defines it?

2. When have you ever failed by your own definition?

3. How do you deal with failure?

4. Can failure be useful? Can you think of times in
your life or somebody else's life when it has led to
something positive?

5. How is failure defined and dealt with in your
family, your school, at work, activities you do outside
of family, school, and work among your friends and
in your community? Which of those definitions and
responses to failure seem fairest or best to you? Why?

6. What can be done to avoid failure?

7. How can people recover from failure?

8. How have you been failed by others?

9. Where do you see failure in society around you?

10. What is the most important lesson I can learn from my failure?

I am certain that after answering these questions as they apply to your situation that it will be quiet evident that you can retrieve some useful lessons from failure or defeat.

Benefits of Defeat

"Before success comes into any man's life he sure to meet with much temporary defeat and perhaps some failures. When defeat overtakes a man, the easiest and the most logical thing to do is to quit. That's exactly what a majority of men do." — Napoleon Hill

In the story of Charles Hew-Len, I could only imagine that after losing his freedom, wife, and kids, he must have felt the sting of failure or defeat. However he would not be where he is today had he not experienced the defeat or failure of prison. There are definitely positive benefits to defeat or failure. Napoleon Hill lists a few of the benefits:

1. May break bad habits and give you the freedom of a fresh start.

2. May remove arrogance and vanity causing you to

do a self inventory to find out what bought on defeat or failure.

3. May lead to a stronger will power.

4. May lead to a deeper sorrow where you may discover spiritual forces not previously recognized.

Kip and Shannon Brooks are a shining example of the benefits that come from tragedy at times they may have felt defeated but decided to practice a positive mental attitude. Kip had experienced a great loss when his previous girlfriend had lost their baby in a previous pregnancy. He wife Shannon was now pregnant with their second baby, when they were made aware that their new baby had a condition known as anencephaly. This is a condition in which most babies are stillborn or do not survive very long after birth.

It was at this critical moment that they would have to decide to go through with the pregnancy or terminate the pregnancy as the doctors were encouraging them to do. They courageously decided to keep the baby and enjoy every precious moment of pregnancy and the birth of their child. Although they knew the outcome they decided to make the most of what seemed to be an unavoidable tragedy. They searched for support groups for other couples that have survived the same dire circumstance. Unfortunately there were none in their area. Their child would only live for 99 minutes after being born, but make a positive impact that would last a life time. Prior to this tragedy, Kip and Shannon's relationship was continually growing more and more distant. Kip was struggling with alcohol addiction that seemed to be getting progressively worse. He had been battling alcohol since he was a teenager, a battle he was losing.

As Napoleon Hill states, "Every defeat, every disappointment and every adversity carry seeds of equivalent benefit." There are several positive benefits that Kip and Shannon experienced, such as the Non Profit, Seasons of Grieve, which they started to support others that are grieving as well from the loss of a child.

Shannon started a greeting card company to express herself and using her creative writing to help other people. The couple found peace and noticed that by helping other people they were healing themselves. Their relationship also benefitted from this tragedy because they became closer in many ways, their marriage is strong and fulfilling because they had to come together to support each other. Some of the keys to overcoming this defeat were that they stayed persistent, didn't stop moving, and refrained from getting caught up in a rut. This amazing couple endured and overcame tragedy, and as a result they are helping to heal grieving people.

Kip is currently an aspiring public speaker and author who use his experience to inspire and heal.

Failure Precedes Greatness

Nothing in this world can take the place of persistence, talent will not: nothing is more common than unsuccessful men with talent. Genius will not; unrewarded genius is almost a proverb. Education will not; the world is full of educated derelicts. Persistence and determination alone are omnipotent. — Calvin Coolidge

Every great politician, writer, entrepreneur, movie star and artist has at some point experienced the sting of defeat and the bitter taste of failure. However, failure became a learning experience that contributed to their success. I have no doubt that you have experienced defeat or failure or tragedy, now you are armed with the knowledge of how to turn your failures around. In fact the failure and defeats are only stop signs on the road to success and proof that you are growing. Please take comfort in my words that you are greater than every circumstance and you will succeed if you persist and don't give up. If so, you will be amongst great company of men who stayed the course until reaching success. Here are a few names that overcame defeat and I believe your name will be right alongside these men, if you don't give up.

1. Isaac Newton: Newton was undoubtedly a genius when it came to math, but he had some failings early on. He never did particularly well in school and when put in charge of running the family farm, he failed miserably, so poorly in fact that an uncle took charge and sent him off to Cambridge where he finally blossomed into the scholar we know today.

2. Henry Ford: While Ford is today known for his innovative assembly line and American-made cars, he wasn't an instant success. In fact, his early businesses failed and left him broke five times before he founded the successful Ford Motor Company.

3. Bill Gates: Gates didn't seem like a shoe-in for success after dropping out of Harvard and starting a failed first business with Microsoft co-founder Paul Allen called Traf-O-Data. While this early idea didn't work, Gates' later work did, creating the global empire that is Microsoft.

4. Winston Churchill: This Nobel Prize-winning, twice-elected Prime Minster of the United Kingdom wasn't always as well regarded as he is today. Churchill struggled in school and failed the sixth grade. After school he faced many years of political failures, as he was defeated in every election for public office until he finally became the Prime Minister at the ripe old age of 62.

5. Abraham Lincoln: While today he is remembered as one of the greatest leaders of our nation, Lincoln's life wasn't so easy. In his youth he went to war a captain and returned a private (if you're not familiar with military ranks, just know that private is as low as it goes.) Lincoln didn't stop failing there, however. He started numerous failed businesses and was defeated in numerous runs he made for public office.

6. Fred Astaire: In his first screen test, the testing director of MGM noted that Astaire, "Can't act. Can't sing. Slightly bald. Can dance a little." Astaire went on to become an incredibly successful actor, singer and dancer and kept that note in his Beverly Hills home to remind him of where he came from.

7. Steven Spielberg: While today Spielberg's name is synonymous with big budget, he was rejected from the University of Southern California School of Theater, Film and Television three times. He eventually attended school at another location, only to drop out to become a director before finishing. Thirty-five years after starting his degree, Spielberg returned to school in 2002 to finally complete his work and earn his BA.

Give failure a new and empowering meaning. Instead of viewing failure as something to be avoided, turn it into a stepping-stone on the path to success. IMPORTANT POINT: Success is the destination. Failure is how you sometimes get there. Welcome failure as a learning experience, sometimes you WIN and sometimes you LEARN.

The Sword

I am the sword standing magnificent a genuine work of art.
Composed of many elements, forged by the fire.
The fires of life have soften me so many times
made me re-hot with weakness and wanting to end my life.
It was at these times I was hit over and over again
by the steel hammer of hardship and trial.
I was at these times it was difficult to smile
The fires of life had put me to the test.
Burning away my impurities
Stripping away my insecurities
Raw elements forged by fire
A heart, burning hot with desire.
Shaped by the environment around me
Doing what I can to sharpen and hone my skills
to put me at the cutting edge of perfection
yet, sometimes dulled by failure and rejection.
Till once again I make that connection
with my master for him I protect and do battle.
On the battlefield of life I am used for defense
On the battlefield under pressure I am at my best
After all this I am dull ready to be honed
This is when my master takes me to the sharpening stone
Now here I am hanging on the wall
The finest piece of weaponry anyone has ever saw
only my master will ever know
the path this cold piece of steel had to go.

-Ralph Cortes III

ABOUT THE AUTHOR: *Ralph Cortes*

Ralph Cortes, a small business owner, entrepreneur, and stepfather, got his start in Chicago, IL. He is presently writing his second book called "Life Outside the Hole." He enjoys a quiet life, far from his action packed days on the street as a gang member, thug, and criminal. Now his days are filled with speaking to inspire youth and teach them about the Napoleon Hill Principles of Success along with several other self-development techniques. Ralph graduated from Southern Illinois University with a degree in Workforce Education and Development with a specialization in education, training and development.

At age 22, in an effort to attain discipline, he honorably served his country as a Sergeant in the United States Marine Corps. There he realized one of his childhood dreams, to be a boxer on the US Marine Corps Boxing Team. Using his curriculum development skills, he has created training for youth at Maryville academy, a group home for abused and neglected youth. Maryville has a special place in Ralph's heart because he used to live there and attributes much of his success to the life skills he learned as a troubled youth at Maryville Academy.

Cortes has three stepchildren from a previous marriage named Sergio, Jlio and Kaila, who were his first long term pupils in youth self development. Ralph realized that he had a gift to connect with children and help to bring out the best in them. His long term goal is to start a Learning Center in which he helps children to develop by teaching them self development techniques. His goal is to make an impact in the world by changing his community one child at a time.

Contact Ralph Cortes at: Ralphc773@gmail.com

Chapter 8

Discover Your Talents

By Fred Grooms

"It had long since come to my attention that people of accomplishment rarely sat back and let things happen to them. They went out and happened to things."
— Leonardo da Vinci

One of Us Is Going to Have to Change

Once again, I found myself sitting alone in the hallway outside my second grade classroom. My arms crossed in defiance and my head hung low with embarrassment. I awaited the inevitable passing student that would certainly call me names and laugh at me once again. Here I sat... unjustly so because I had only spoken out of turn when I mistakenly heard the teacher call my name.

"Get ready," she says. What I heard in my excitement was, "OK, Freddy."

I shouted out the answer with great enthusiasm! Even though my answer was correct, my action was met with disapproval. You see, I didn't often know the answer to any of the questions my teacher was asking of the class. This helps you understand my excitement.

It only took a few moments for the first of several fourth graders to pass by me in the hallway, taking the opportunity to giggle on their way back from the library. A few moments later the assistant principal collected me up and took me to the office where I heard a familiar speech. A lecture would be more accurate. She told me about how I needed to behave, that my booger jokes and armpit noises weren't funny, and no one liked the class clown.

"But I thought she called my name," I insisted. "I had the answer to her question. She's just being mean."

Her response, "Freddy, your teacher didn't send you out into the hall to be mean."

"Yes, she did!" I shouted. "I hate school!"

The assistant principal picked up the phone to call my mother, yet again, to express her displeasure. Surely, this was not going to go over well with my mother, let alone my father. There was no need to proclaim my innocence because no one was going to listen. I would just sit in silence and allow my dislike for school to grow.

I had been in the principal's office before. Being sent to sit in the hallway was unfortunately not new. I was there for offences described earlier, for making jokes, for talking out of turn, or for not participating. School and I just didn't get along.

School was like jail. They structured every moment of my time. School required me to conform to the rules, to sit down, be still, be quiet, listen and learn. All I wanted to do was move around, ask questions, get answers other than "because", and be allowed to show what I had learned.

One of us was going to have to change to survive. Guess who?

"Face the facts of being what you are, for that is what changes what you are."
— Soren Kierkgaard

Fearing Change

I've grown to have a love and hate relationship with change. Like so many of us, I hate change especially when someone else is forcing change upon me.

We hate change because we fear change. Change requires us to put forth effort to do things differently. We find ourselves outside our comfort zones fearing what we have not experienced, and afraid of the anticipated pain change might bring.

Change is a departure from the past. It requires us to leave what is familiar and comfortable. Changing jobs, graduating school, or moving to a new city requires us to leave what and who we know. In a real sense it requires us to mourn our loss.

We fear the failure that change could bring. No one wants to come up short on their goals or dreams so it's easier to just sit on the sidelines of life being comfortable right where we are. We come up with excuses as to why we need not even try to change, saying things like, "It's just a waste of time," "It doesn't really matter anyway," or "What I do isn't really going to accomplish anything."

Our society has adopted the maxim, "Failure is not an option." By doing so we stop people from even trying to change and be successful. What we should be doing is realizing that each failure brings us closer to success. The problem is whenever failure is not option, we cease trying.

This is precisely where I found myself through most of my early education, even though I wasn't able to articulate my feelings at the time. If I wasn't going to be perfect, why even try?

I wasn't like other kids. I didn't feel smart. Reading, writing, and math were difficult for me. Everyone else was getting A's and I wasn't, and I resented them. Everyone seemed to be talented at something except for me.

The school system just didn't know what to do with me. I had an IQ that said I was too smart to be "special." Yet, I didn't seem to have the drive or skill to keep up with my classmates.

Upon further investigation, it was determined I have the learning disability known as dyslexia. Being dyslexic meant special education classes, and having to repeat the second grade. Being diagnosed as a dyslexic set me on a path of deficit remediation. The system was going to "fix" my weakness and change me. Unfortunately, the system failed. The system wasn't necessarily at fault, but being dyslexic isn't something that is fixable. With a great deal of effort on my part and tremendous amount of support from my parents and teachers I did learn to read, write, and do math.

Regrettably, our educational system's reliance upon the deficit remediation approach for fixing weaknesses has changed little over the years. In fact it has fine-tuned its ability to identify, categorize, label, and track deficits.

The Weakness Trap

Professional educators call fixing your weaknesses the deficit-based remediation approach. Our educational system is certainly not alone in its fixation upon fixing your weaknesses. Corporations work to fix your weaknesses, and want you to change so you conform to their norms and their specifications. Companies accomplish this through employee evaluations, or coaching up. Even in our closest relationships we try to change each other all the time. No matter the name, it all boils down to you spending most of your energy on fixing what others believe is broken about you. Most people in your life will want to force you to change.

It's the Weakness Trap. The weakness trap is the unhealthy and unproductive obsession with focusing on changing weaknesses. What is wanted from you is to work harder and harder at what you're not any good at so you can move from being bad at something to be... not bad at something. How does this make sense, considering the time and effort it takes?

As a dyslexic I could spend years trying to master the rules of grammar and spelling. At some point, I could perhaps be good at it but at what cost to other areas in my life where I am naturally talented?

I was in my sophomore year in high school when I finally had enough of people trying to change me, and fix my weaknesses. I insisted on being allowed to take classes I was interested in and stop all the remedial crap.

I got my wish. I soon realized that I was on my own to make it or fail. I did manage to graduate high school and was even able to talk my way into college. It was later in college that I realized I was in fact talented.

"It may be hard for an egg to turn into a bird: it would be a jolly sight harder for it to learn to fly while remaining an egg. We are like eggs at present. And you cannot go on indefinitely being just an ordinary, decent egg. We must be hatched or go bad."
— C.S. Lewis

Discovering Talents

Wouldn't it be great if as a society we invested time, any time at all would be a start, teaching people to identify their natural talents? Shouldn't people be taught to become more of who they already are, rather than conforming to someone else's vision of who they should be? I envision a world that departs from the weakness trap and focuses on the realization that everyone is uniquely talented. Everyone is talented. You may not have been raised to believe in your talents, but you have them.

The problem with recognizing talent is all too often there is a narrow view of what it means to be talented. Must one be able to sing, dance, play an instrument, create lavish art work, or be a sports star to be talented? If you can't do those things, this doesn't mean that you are not talented. Many are raised with a narrow view of what it means to be talented. Many are brought up to think that only the arts, music, and sports equal talents, and fortunately, this just isn't true.

Understand that everyone is a unique creation. There is no one in the world like you. There might be someone who looks like you, but they are not you, nor will there ever be another you. Think about how amazing that is. Out of the billions of people there are right now, have ever been, or ever will be, you are 100 percent unique. You are talented, smart, beautiful, and yes, you matter.

Each and every person has been given specific talents. Some may call them gifts. With these talents or gifts come the responsibility to use them in service to yourself, and especially to others. Those who can identify their talents are much more likely to make a major impact on others.

Talents are an individual's core personality traits, and are unlikely to change over time. Talents are our natural way of thinking, feeling and behaving.

Identify Your Talents by Asking Questions. Here are a few simple questions that will get you thinking about your talents.

• If someone would pay you to do anything what would you do?

• Think about how you react to crisis, are you calm, cool and collected? Do your respond by taking a step back and analyzing the situation?

• When faced with a difficult decision do you gather

information or do you make a command decision?

• Are you spontaneous or do you prefer to weigh all the options?

• How do you deal with relationships? Are you someone who loves to collect friends or are you more interested in deep relationships?

• Do you pray?

All of these questions will help you discover your talents. Natural talents are literally what you do without any effort. Your talents empower you. They make it possible for you to move to higher levels of excellence and fulfill your potential. Researchers tell us that most often your highest achievements will be linked to your greatest talents.

Name Your Talents

It's important to name and claim your individual talents. Name your talents, not just identify them. What's the difference? There is a great deal of power behind giving something a name.

Think of it this way. Someone can stand on a hillside and look down upon the lush green vegetation and call it a forest. A forest is full of trees. We can identify a tree by its bark, leaves, height, and structure, but until you give it a name it's just another tree. When you name the tree as a Giant Redwood then the tree has all the majestic power of a Giant Redwood.

Being able to name your talents is no different. Naming your talents gives you a language to describe what you know about yourself and it makes talents real. Naming your talents will empower you. Once you can give your talents a name you can then begin to invest in developing them into strengths.

Since so much time has been spent focusing on weakness it will take time to discover and uncover your natural talent. It takes detective work and self-reflection on your part. It will also take training.

There are two primary sources I would recommend that you investigate to assist you in discovering your talents. Both resources are web-based talent and strengths assessments. The first is StrengthsFinder 2.0 produced by Gallup. This assessment has been taken by nearly nine million people.

The second is the Values In Action Survey or VIA. This is strictly an online web-based assessment. Take time to invest in naming your talents through one of these assessments.

"Change in all things is sweet" — Aristotle

Embracing Change

My love affair with change is about the infinite possibilities associated with what is next. Change can be about opportunities not yet discovered. Change is most always energizing and can empower us to amazing greatness.

It's been said that change makes us smarter, and I certainly agree. Without change there is no progress in our lives. It is easy to become so comfortable so as to settle for living lives that are average and mediocre. In all my years working with students, I have yet to meet one whose life goals and dreams were about being average. But I have seen how we allow the fear of change to paralyze us into living lives of weakness and just becoming average.

With nearly three decades of experience in leadership, education, coaching, and training it's been my greatest pleasure to see people embrace change. They break free from the weakness trap of always focusing on what's broken about them. This allows them to shift that focus and energy to their unique talents. To invest in others is to assist them in the creation of true personal strengths. When this happens, motivation skyrockets, overall productivity increases, relationships get stronger, and happiness is possible. Who doesn't want to be happier?

Some of us are going to have to change to survive, will it be you?

ABOUT THE AUTHOR: *Fred Grooms*

I am the owner of Barnabas Consulting, and the founder of Strengths Development. We work with educators and students in middle school through college. It's our goal to assist students to become more of who they already are. We teach students and staff to identify and invest in their personal talents and strengths. It's also vital that we teach students to understand the role their talents and strengths play in the choices and decisions they make.

I'm passionate about reaching students. I speak at school assemblies, student leadership organizations, and conferences. My team works with college and university student services, guidance, college and career placement services and leadership groups, just to name a few. I lead workshops and seminars on talent and strengths development, and on making quality life and career choices.

As mentioned earlier, I graduated high school, although at the bottom of my class. I talked my way into North Georgia College, a Senior Military College. I earned my degree in business management. One of the proudest moments of my life was earning my commission as an officer in the US Army, and serving for five years on active duty attaining the rank of Captain. Over the years

I have attained a number of advanced degrees and certifications.

It has always be my passion to serve others, whether serving my country, working to create new business units in the private business sector, or working for non-profits.

My passion for serving others grew and I was called to students. I served as a youth and children's pastor for 15 years. It was in the in this position I came to realize that many students were struggling to find their place in a world focused on weakness.

Today, my calling is to teach others, and specifically students, to understand they are uniquely created. That everyone has talents, and gifts to be shared with those around them and thus the world.

Join me, as we teach students and individuals to be more of who they already are. Recognize your own strengths. Realize your own unique talents. Lead with this! And then teach others the same!

Fred
www.fredgrooms.com
www.strengthsdevelopment.com
www.fredoncampus.com

Chapter 9

Looking for Health in One Drop of Blood

By Denise Abda

I was very sick in the 1980s, after my child was born. What happened for me was a journey back to the garden. I transformed my own health by changing what I put inside my body. This was not the only transformation I was to experience, however.

The start of my consciousness awakening was 2003. I felt before that time I was asleep. I didn't know that I was asleep, though, until things started happening in my life. Suddenly the things I began to think about started to manifest. They were too coincidental to be coincidences.

For more than 30 years I had worked in blood, in the medical industry, taking blood for people and analyzing that blood.

Then, when I began to awaken, I kept seeing things that I thought about manifesting in my life. It's almost like I would open up the newspaper, and see a picture of a person featured, and that person would walk in the door an hour later. Now with seven billion people on the planet, this could not have been a coincidence.

As my life became more and more guided, I realized that when I was able to pay attention, I could manifest everything I was thinking or dreaming about.

I believe that when people begin to allow themselves to be guided, miracles happen. Answers show up to the questions you ask.

Suddenly, as part of my awakening, I began to see new things in the blood that I was analyzing as part of my job as a medical technologist. I would take blood out of people's arms and put it into machines, and get back numbers. All those numbers would come back, but the people were all different and the numbers weren't telling the whole story. In fact, some people who were very sick would have normal numbers on their testing (or numbers within a range determined to be normal). So the imaging and the numbers weren't making sense.

So this gave me an awakening around blood and what good healthy blood looks like, and how the numbers don't always tell the story. In fact, the numbers can lie.

The insight I was having at this time was that in an

evolutionary sense, we all have more work to do. That my purpose on the planet could well be to help people understand how to have healthy blood, and to focus not just on the numbers, but on health itself and what a healthy blood cell looks like.

So now I was blessed with a journey around the power of nutrition, and my own 30 years of experience at looking at blood cells. I began to read everything I could about nutrition. It started working! I was joyful, because I was able to heal myself when I changed what went into my body.

So now I am committed to teaching people how your blood is really a way of looking at your entire life. Without circulation, your blood cannot get through your body. Blood patterns indicate where acids are in the body.

The central cause of most sickness is too much acid in the body. Acids settle in weak genetics, and that is how genetics are damaged. Understanding this, the way of health, as I see it, is to become more alkaline. A Nobel Prize winner, Otto Warburg, found that cancer lives and thrives in an acid environment.

So to turn around where cancer lives (in an acid environment), alkaline environments breed health and it is my belief that cancer does not grow in that environment. I teach people how to become more alkaline to keep the pH of your systems up.

Health is really easy. You can transform your entire body by changing the blood and its flow and its contents. I teach people to start each day with a healthy green shake.

This all comes down to looking at blood under the microscope. When you watch it long enough, you can observe what it does. What happens for me is that I can see blood changing when people I help begin to change what they put inside of their bodies. Here are steps you can take to transform your life, and feel more health, every day. If you can't make all of the changes at one time, change one thing every few weeks until your life transforms itself over the course of a year.

Step 1: Begin with a healthy mindset. Trust that you can change, and health is possible. Trust that you will be guided to do the right things to turn your body into a healthy place. So many people become fearful when they are sick. Fear begets more fear, begets more illness. So let go of the fear.

Step 2: Be open to a healing therapy that may not be what you thought. Open your mind to the possibilities of what is right for you. Begin to trust that bigger part of you that knows. When you don't let the fear in, you have freedom to make choices. See if you can let fear (and its power to freeze you) go and replace it with a sense of adventure. What is possible? Ask this.

For me, I became present to the power of alternative therapies when I was sick after my pregnancy. I learned from masters how to change what went inside of my body, and this had nothing to do with drugs or the medical institutions. This had a profound change on my world view. I got to health through nutrition, and I believe in this now with all of my heart and soul.

Step 3: Begin to eat more greens. Eat live and raw foods. Change your PH. Go through the detoxification process. Diseases are toxins that are built up in the body. I watch the blood in the body, and I support people in making changes so the blood can reflect more health, less disease.

One simple way to change your diet is to shop the perimeter in a grocery store. Shop for the live, green, real food and shift away from processed or frozen foods. You'll notice that the food that is on the perimeter of the store is always the freshest food. This will bring your blood cells health and vitality.

Step 4: Recognize there may be an emotional component to your disease or lack of health. See if you can identify the emotional component and release that. I'm working with a woman who was married for 40 years. She had liver cancer. About three months before she found out about the cancer, she found out her husband had cheated on her. Her cells turned hard and a tumor was built. All her cells settled into a hard liver and I could see a connection with the expression of anger. Every time she would look at him, she would feel angry, and she could not forgive. I don't know if she will heal. She is learning to forgive. He is grateful she is forgiving and is learning to appreciate her. I'm not sure if she can heal, because she is so settled in her anger. We work on the alkalinity in her body, and changing her pH. But she has to release the anger, not because of him, but for her own body's well-being.

As you eat and drink and think, look at how you are thinking, and look at what you are eating. When your thoughts are acid, this harbors in your body. Everything will be done to help this woman, but it is hard to say if she can let go of all of that anger and pain that is manifesting itself as cancer inside of her body.

Step 5: Exercise and Oxygenate Your Body. Movement is vital to health. Movement is how we can bring oxygen into the body. The body needs to utilize oxygen correctly. Otherwise it doesn't have enough oxygen coming through circulation, so fermentation occurs. Then, the environment isn't suitable for health and wellness.

If you can't exercise in a big way, you can use oxygen drops. But see about bringing more oxygen into your body and see about moving your body. Start small if you need to start small.

I met with a woman recently who had terrible postpartum depression and was on anti-depressants for 12 years. We looked at what she eats and drinks during the day. We started to talk through it. She wants to be done with medication.

She is taking medication, but she is still depressed. So she knows that she needs to find a new way of approaching her health. I offered to look at her blood under microsopy, and this had a huge impact. When people see their blood under a microscope, and I explain what the images mean, this changes people.

So with this young woman (about 41) she first began to hydrate. She needs to drink more water. Everyone needs to drink a lot of water! This helps toxins flow out, and helps everything work better.

So as we look at her blood, she felt an inkling of hope. I gave her an easy recipe for a green shake in the morning to get started. She begins to exercise, and hydrate, and eat alkaline foods. I allowed her blood to talk to me and tell me what it needed for a healthier way of being. We recognized that in the morning, as she got out of bed, her blood is stuck. When her blood is stuck, not moving, still, her kidneys are not getting what they need. Her brain is not getting blood flow. Her heart is not pumping blood through her body in a healthy way.

She started just by drinking more water, and she is adding good stuff to put into her body. She has a green shake, some healthy minerals, some healthy vitamins. She is able to go off of her medication, and she loses weight. She feels better about her life, and this changes how she is able to parent her children. Healthy blood changes everything.

Step 6: Don't ever lose hope. Stay in faith that all the right things will show up when you need them. Trust that health is possible no matter how bad things are.

Step 7: Never succumb to the system. So what if you have had a bad diagnosis. You need to look at one cell of your blood, and see if you can influence health in one cell. Influence your health by putting the right things into your body, and influence your health by moving your body. You need to let go of emotional pain, this is weighing you down.

Just know that help is possible, and health is possible. It all begins with your blood.

ABOUT THE AUTHOR: *Denise Abda, MT(ASCP), IMA, HC(AADP)*

Denise Abda worked through the traditional healthcare system for 25+ years as a clinical laboratory medical technologist. She holds a BS in Biochemistry from the University of Scranton and an accreditation from the Americal Society of Clinical Pathology (ASCP). She furthered her education by studying the acid alkaline balance approach to health and also graduated from The Institute of Integrative Nutrition in NYC where she earned certification from The American Association of Drugless Practitioners (AADP). She completed certifications in Matrix Energetics, German New Medicine and Chiren Light Therapy.

Her expertise of over 20 years in the wellness industry began after she exhausted traditional therapies for her own health challenges. Through research into nutrition and lifestyle choices in health and healing she provides support and wellness education programs customized to your unique needs

Contact Denise Abda at www.DeniseAbda.com
PO Box 623
Clarks Summit, PA 18411
570-561-5063
YpHBalance@yahoo.com

Chapter 10

Boldly Cure Your Ailments

By Donna LaBar

My 12-year-old daughter Monica and I clung together sobbing as the oncologist quietly left Monica's hospital room. We thought Monica had a strange virus that she couldn't shake. Two months went by and my once athletic, witty, practical jokester slowly melted into a world of 24-hour care, blood tests, and IVs. Now we knew what it was. It had a name and with that came the horrifying truth of how life can change in an instant.

Monica was diagnosed on November 24, 1998, with Acute Myloid Leukemia, AML. She went from complaining of hip and joint pain in the summer, to flu-like symptoms in early October, to total hospitalization by the end of November. Receiving the diagnosis went something like this: "Monica, you have a cancer of your blood that is very aggressive. It appears you have had it for three to six months. It has shown itself to be a terminal cancer in the elderly population. We can give you chemotherapy, large doses, like a sledge hammer to your system. You may not make it through the first two weeks of this treatment. We believe at this stage you may have two weeks to live without treatment. In addition, you also have a blood-clotting disorder, which makes taking chemotherapy very dangerous. We must try to establish if your ability to clot can be corrected or chemotherapy is not an option. I will be sending in members of our team to talk about all of this with you and your Mom."

Then the doctor quietly exits the room.

Back up to my late teen years. In September 1975, I get a co-operative education job through my school in a school-to-work program. I had been a business major in high school and was happy to get a job as a starter legal secretary for a local law firm. I was there about a year when they hired a new attorney, fresh out of law school, and she and I became fast friends. I lived in northern rural Pennsylvania and she had grown up in West Chester, just outside of Philadelphia.

On weekends, we would make the trek to visit her parents.

They were eclectic couple. She had been a nurse but left the field to raise their children and he was a chemical engineer. I will call them Jo and Al. They enjoyed their gardens, reading and the art of conversation. We quickly became friends. They helped me create a huge lovely rock garden and taught me a lot about botanicals. A few years into the friendship, Al was experiencing illness and was diagnosed with stomach cancer. He was around 60 years old at the time. They quickly determined that he needed to have his stomach removed. Of course, there weren't many alternatives 30 years ago, so he went for the surgery even though the prognosis was not encouraging.

He made it through the surgery and decided to use his knowledge of chemistry and apply it to healing himself. With the normal digestion process unavailable, taking enzymes and supplements became a way of life in order to get proper nutrition. Jo helped him with her interest in natural foods and cooking. During this time, I became close to Al and was totally intrigued by his studies and discoveries regarding nutritional and natural healing.

He was like a mad scientist, and I was the inquisitive apprentice. He would come up with recipes and formulas for things that would correct illnesses, mostly for his friends and family. I would help him in his quest to find products that were already on the market that were similar to his original recipes so we could direct friends where to find something that would help them. I learned so much and started to maintain my health with holistic approaches. I would research different opinions, data and studies, and would discuss them with Al, always looking for that which made the most sense and that which was the most reasonable approach for the common individual. Al taught me so much and lived a wonderful full life, just passing on recently at the age of 93.

My fascination with natural healing and the discoveries I had with Al about the body's abilities to repair itself were part of my life for 20 years or so by the time Monica was ill. The purpose for my inquisitive studies and passion for alternative healing quickly snapped into focus with her cancer diagnosis. I worked with her oncologists combining conventional treatment with alternative approaches. We left no stone unturned. Monica and I tried many different things to help her mind, body and spirit during this time. We believed she could make it through this, not easily, but still attainably, just one day at a time. She would be our miracle. She healed, and is alive today, quite vibrant and in her 20s.

I hold the strong belief in healing, and in healing miracles.

There have been, not just one, but millions of cases of miraculous healing documented through the centuries! So why can't that be you? If you were suddenly scratched today, in a few days the scratch would be scabbed over and in a few weeks it would for the most part be gone. This is part of the miracle - the body not only can heal itself, healing is truly a part of its design!

Supporting the body's complex bio chemical ability to heal is not difficult, in fact it's easy!

Your body does all the complicated stuff automatically when given the right ingredients.

Start today. Your body will gladly cooperate. After all, if you give it exactly what it needs when it needs it, you will never find anything on the planet that operates as keenly and efficiently as the human body. Our body, with over 50 trillion cells, will completely replace every cell in a year. The body has the amazing ability to maintain a temperature of 98.6 degrees, maintain an alkaline/acid pH balance of 7.365, regulate blood sugar levels, regulate fluids, make enzymes and hormones, digest and absorb nutrients to nourish cells, regenerate healthy cells, anticipate what is good and bad for us, plus remove toxins and waste. The body is fully equipped to recover from illness or injury and heal itself. The most amazing pharmacy is the human body!

Our health is influenced by three environments which we provide. The first environment is built by the food we eat to nourish our cells to maintain normal body functions. Second, the thoughts we think that either make us feel great or make us ill. And, third, our surroundings, where we live, work, play and create. Our choices and how, good or bad, they predict much of our health experiences and future.

How we nourish the body is very important in relation to what it has to offer back to us for mental and physical leverage. Like a computer: garbage in, garbage out. We must have some basic knowledge of good maintenance for the body to get the most out of it. It's exciting for me to provide some cool information that has helped many people make all difference in their lives!

One very important fact that few know about is that our body needs to maintain a pH balance between 7.35 and 7.45 in order to remain healthy. When we are born our body is alkaline and as we are exposed to the elements like food, environment and stresses, the body can become acidic. This simple fact is one of the most common reasons we see so much illness today. Once the body drops below 7, an acidic state, health begins to decline and eventually disease is present. This process can be slow and goes from a state of just uncomfortable bouts of inflammation, heartburn or acid reflux, insomnia, etc. , in which case the individual will take over-the-counter drugs such as pain killers, stomach and digestive aids, stool softeners and laxatives or sleep aids. Eventually, it will be necessary to step the process of decline to the level of more complex medicines from a doctor for worsening symptoms. The person doesn't look at their diet or lifestyle or thoughts at this point, they just consider this normal non-life threatening health issues or a stage of aging. As the body continues with no sustenance for maintaining normal alkaline/acid levels, inflammatory issues ensue and diseases like cancer, diabetes, MS, lupus, arthritis, fibromyalgia, etc. become common diagnosis.

Cancer for instance does not grow in an alkaline base, however it does grow easily in an acidic environment. It is my belief that if an individual is trying to prevent or slow an ailment or disease, or is receiving treatment for cancer, it is very important to provide the body with a diet that is 75 percent alkaline foods and 25 percent acid foods to support the body through the process to recovery. This can be as easy as looking at an alkaline/acid food chart and making choices that leave your plate filled with 75 percent of alkaline- forming foods you have chosen and 25 percent of acid- forming foods. There is a basic alkaline/acid food chart available on my website, www.DonnaLa-Bar.com, to help you make this assessment. Alkaline foods are not necessarily known with basic common sense, so a chart will be helpful until you are comfortable. For instance, a lemon is acidic in its natural state, however, once ingested becomes alkaline-forming and is therefore and excellent choice. On the other hand, a banana is alkaline in its natural state because of its high potassium content, however, becomes acid-forming once ingested because of its' high sugar content.

Alkalinity in the body happens as a result of the mineral content in our foods. The primary minerals that have an alkalizing effect are calcium, iron, magnesium, manganese and potassium. In order to support the body to keep the alkaline state, eating foods rich in the primary minerals is the key. These minerals are all very important for pH balance and all of them have different health benefits. It is imperative to have a diet rich in plant-based, low sugar content foods to provide the balance needed for the proper function of all of our organs and natural healing. Our complex bio chemical system creates our enzymes and hormones, fluctuates our fluids, runs our organs and repairs and replaces cells non-stop, gets what it needs to perform from our food and water.

If you are curious to know where you stand, buy a pack of alkaline test strips for urine testing. Tear off a strip and dip it in your urine stream and check the color it turns again the chart provided with the strips. Generally a yellow strip reveals acidic urine and a medium/dark green color strip is alkaline. It is best to check urine as opposed to saliva because it's best to test after the body has ingested the food.

I mentioned environments that influence our alkaline/acid balance. Your food choices do have a huge impact on health and so do your thoughts. Anxious thoughts and worry naturally make the body produce cortisol and adrenaline. These secretions are acidic. If this state becomes constant, or a way of life, the individual can experience acidity and possibly hormonal problems in spite of a good diet. Another place that acidity can show up in spite of a good diet is through extreme exercise. I have read about soda doping, where an athlete will drink water with baking soda (sodium bicarbonate) to get their lactic acid level down after an extreme demand on their body from physical exercise. It is said that it can have a significant effect on endurance and speed due to the alkalizing effect of the blood pH. The goal of all of this is to create and support the perfect environment in our body to function properly. This supports our body's ability to utilize and produce enzymes.

Without Enzymes We Would Not Be Alive

 Enzymes, without them, we would not be alive. We need them to eat and breathe.
Our body does produce a staggering number of different types of enzymes, which is awesome, except it does not do this indefinitely and especially without the right conditions. A poor diet and accelerated aging can cause the decline in the body's ability to produce enzymes. The more conscious a person is about getting enzymes in their diet, the more healthy and energetic they become. Enzyme richness will dramatically slow the aging process and the progression of disease.

When food is cooked beyond 116 degrees Fahrenheit, the enzymes are destroyed in the process. Eating uncooked, unprocessed food is the best way to ensure your body is getting a steady supply of enzymes. Having enzymes active in food allows it to digest easily without as much work for the body because the food contains the necessary enzymes for digestion. A change as simple as being mindful to eat a live component with every meal will quickly improve digestion, reduce acid and provide better elimination. As a result of improving the digestive process, you are rewarded with more energy and increased mental clarity. The great news is that you experience all of this fairly quickly. The body responds graciously when it has the right materials to work with.

There is a caveat to this, not all foods can be utilized for their full nutritional potential without being cooked. For instance, carbohydrates (starches) are a good example. In the cooking process, the starch molecule is broken down with heat and water, called gelatinization, making it more enjoyable and easier for the body to get nutrients from it. Foods like grains, root vegetables, corn, dried beans and peas become edible and provide absorbable nutrients by being cooked. The body creates the enzymes necessary for the digestion of these carbohydrates. It may be necessary to supplement with digestive enzymes if your body has trouble digesting foods that are important in your diet. Since enzymes not only help with digestion and absorption, they also assist in elimination, it is imperative we get enzymes in some fashion to support our health.

The Importance of Elimination (Good Poop)

I mentioned elimination and I can't responsibly discuss proper digestion without covering the importance of removing waste and toxins from the body as steadily and as regularly as we put food in for nourishment. The best rule of thumb I believe is that you should have a bowel movement after each meal, so you may go three times a day or more. It's important not to have prolonged diarrhea or constipation as neither is normal and both can lead to serious illness. With diarrhea, crucial nutrients may not be absorbed during digestion leaving the body malnourished in spite of the fact that you are eating regularly. Constipation can be equally debilitating. The waste after digestion and inhalation is full of bacteria, toxins and pollutants that need to exit regularly.

Constipation is a condition created when the body, dehydrated, pulls all of the fluid out of the waste or stool to use in our blood and lymph system to maintain the amount of fluid necessary to function. It's a survival skill on the part of the resourceful body responding to the immediate crisis. Of course this fluid is septic and a poor source of fluid in the long term. Without proper hydration, this can go on for a long time and slowly deteriorating your health.

Proper hydration and fiber in the diet is so important for the elimination process. Keeping the body hydrated so it can pump blood to the organs and toxins can clear through our lymphatic system is vital. Fiber helps the waste to move on through the body and is eliminated with ease. A constant supply of water intake and good roughage at meal times will keep these matters in check or keep you "regular" as the saying goes. It may be necessary to create new routines that include keeping fresh water close by at all times. I have found that I easily drink water all day with a supply with me in my car and at my desk. Not hydrating leaves you feeling very tired by the afternoon. When I'm feeling sluggish it's my natural alarm that my body is low on fluids, I reach for a big glass of water and amazingly get energized.

Balancing Your Blood Sugar

Another diet related issue with energy is the roller coaster ride your blood sugar takes if your diet is not balanced. A balanced diet consists of carbohydrates, proteins and fats. Proteins and fats allow the body to create tissue and insulation, so you must eat some lean protein and healthy fats. Carbohydrates provide calories used to make energy. The energy produced from carbohydrates is used for our normal everyday body functions like movement, heartbeat, breathing and digesting. There are two categories of carbohy-drates, simple and complex.

Simple carbohydrates get there name because they are simple sugars that do not have a lot of nutri-tional value, digest quickly and therefore enter the bloodstream fast. Some examples of simple carbs are table sugar, white flour and any products with these ingredients as well as honey, molasses, jelly, jam, fruit juices, fruit, flavored yogurts, chocolate, soda and packaged cereals, just to name a few of the most popular. The fast pace of current times have left most of the population chasing their energy slumps throughout the day with caffeine and simple carbohydrates. This is the ride that takes you to the bad lands!

Caffeine gives the adrenaline rush and simple sugars quickly raise your blood sugar for a short time leaving you feeling awake and charged for an instant; then the big descend to low blood sugar, which leaves you extremely tired and wanting a big nap. You can easily get off this ride. Eliminate simple carbohydrates, they are energy thieves! Your addiction to caffeine will gradually disappear as the experience of intense fatigue from swaying blood sugar is eliminated. In addition to the feeling of exhaustion, huge peeks and valley with blood sugar is just the start of sliding down a slippery slope with your health. Obesity, pre diabetes and diabetes are out of control in many societies, a huge problem for the United States. Avoiding simple carbs and becoming mindful of how you feel when you eat, will bring you closer to enjoying solid, stable good health. Food should make you feel charged nor exhausted. Start paying attention, being mindful of how you feel a half hour after a meal or snack.

Complex carbohydrates on the other hand are important in our diet and act as fuel and give us energy. They have a more complex chemical makeup, a complex of sugars made up of fiber, minerals and vitamins. Complex carbs take longer to digest so they enter the blood slower, and do not cause the ups and downs in energy of simple carbohydrates. Complex carbs are found in vegetables and whole grains, examples of them are beans, broccoli, celery, legumes, lentils, spinach, yams and zucchini. Complex carbs give you the most bang for your buck so to speak. You can eat them in abundance without adding a lot of calories, and they provide loads of vitamins and nutrients along with more hydration and fiber to aid in digestion and elimination. Our spark or energy is fueled by enzymes, minerals and water. Your diet should be loaded with alkaline complex carbohydrates. This will keep your light shining brightly.

Experiencing Happiness

Enjoying happiness and feeling optimistic should be a normal part of life. We are meant to live in harmony and cooperation, not competing and fighting. Part of our internal health is what we eat but the other half is what we think. As I mentioned earlier, we have three environments that influence our health. Eating properly is half the battle, but thinking healthy is another huge element to wellness. Bad thoughts, worrying and monkey mind bring on stress, anxiety, sadness and sometimes depression. All of this is extremely hard on your body. When you are stressed the body automatically creates hormones to deal with this threatening information the body senses. That is our fight or flight response, still keenly in place as part of our complex bodily functions to protect us from danger.

Now you don't need this to flee from dinosaurs as our ancestors did, but it does signal you every single time that something feels wrong, sounds wrong or smells wrong to you. If you could just become aware of what makes you happy and what makes you sad or frightened, then simply embrace more of the first and avoid the later, you would be doing a momentous boost to every cell in your body and would make a significant improvement in your overall health and life. Some professionals do muscle testing, applied kinesiology, to see if your body tests weak or strong to a product, idea or question. This is an amazing way to experience how your body instinctively knows what it believes is good for it and what is bad.

Getting in touch with this and beginning to honor yourself by acknowledging what does not make you happy and correcting this is just as important as you being mindful to eat healthier to feel the energy that is provided by your food, thus make this connection of how what is in your mind and body can fuel you or make you wilt. It may be as simple as starting to say no to things or people that no longer support or serve who you are and what makes you hum along nicely.

Addressing these issues can be equally or more diffi-cult than getting rid of the morning java with a bagel, but the rewards are staggering and a must if you are going to enjoy total wellness. Once you have commit-ted to solve the hardest issues, so many things will fall into place automatically. You will feel better, so you will eat better and exercise willingly, relax more and sleep peacefully. This is the cycle to strive for.

Good Sleep

Sleeping really well and waking up refreshed is an imperative part of healthy living. When you sleep, a nice full, long, uninterrupted sleep, your body heals and repairs itself. This is the important part of the equation that helps keep you from illness and disease as well as giving you prolonged youthfulness and a creative active mind. When the mind and the diet are a mess, good sleep can become impossible. You must work through this and there are many things to try. You may need to try them all, but don't stop until you have conquered any sleep troubles you have.

First, make sure you are tired! Just being exhausted mentally isn't enough to get you a good night of sleep, you need to be physically tired as well. Even if you are not mentally exhausted, you should get physical exercise to promote good sleeping. Get in the habit of at least a walk in the morning, at lunchtime or after dinner. The more aggressive the stroll you take the better. Breathe in fully to force good oxygen into your cells and stretch a bit too if you think of it. All of this gets you a valuable good sleep with a fresher feeling when you wake. Don't avoid a chance to do physical work, our lives have become way to sedentary. Take the stairs, run to the post office, in fact run your errands! We say we are out to run our errands, but we always take the car! Push yourself whenever you can. Use it or lose it -- they were not kidding. Remember, you are doing all of this for delicious healthy sleep and total overall wellness.

The most typical things to help sleep are to take a warm bath in Epsom salts and a bit of baking soda and relax with soft light and music. Clear your mind and prepare for a good night of rest. It may also help to have an herb tea that is offered as a sleep aid such as chamomile tea, or warm milk with a hint of nutmeg (my grandmother's favorite). Minerals such as calcium and magnesium also help with sleep. Taking your calcium with magnesium supplement at bedtime is good for sleeping and also providing your body with minerals to assist in the repair of your body during slumber.

Other supplements like melatonin or 5-htp can also be helpful. The choice of vitamin or vitamins can depend on your reason for insomnia. Melatonin is the most well known for helping people get rest. It is a hormone that your body may slow or quit making cause trouble with your internal clock. The dosage really can vary a lot depending on the individual. It's best to start with a small dosage and work your way up if you are trying this supplement. If you are not taking enough, you may experience vivid dreams or even nightmares, so you will know if you need more. If you wake up short of a full night of sleep take another and it will ease you back to sleep easily. The

5-htp is the precursor to L-tryptophan which raises the serotonin level. It makes you feel better overall and helps calm your mind. I know individuals that take 50 to 100 mg in the morning and 50 to 100 mg at night and this seems to steady them through their day and give them a peaceful night of sleep.

One of my favorites is reading to get ready to sleep. I also like listening to an audio book, and sometimes I use headset to tune into vibrational beats and tones to help me get into a deep sleep. If you are a poor sleeper, don't give up. Keep making the necessary changes in your life to get the rest you need. It may take a few changes or many, take just one step at a time.

Making Changes

A change is usually the right medicine for many areas of your life even though it may seem like the toughest solution. We have covered changing the diet and changing your thoughts, but ultimately health may require changing your environment. Where we live, where we work and who we spend that time with has an effect on our life and health. Now this can be tremendously good, and you know right now if it is or not. So you may want to start by just looking around, thinking to yourself, what gives me joy here and what makes me anxious or causes me pain. Again, expand and bring more into your life that brings joy and start minimizing or changing that that makes you weak.

There are many ways to do this as well. Start out with the realization that you have the ability to identify these areas and then make choices to change is all within your power and scope. The changes can start truly with just your awareness of wanting to work toward joy and peace in your life. The rest can be slow and subtle but all in a direction of honoring who you are and finding joy for yourself. This does not have to be at another's expense. Ultimately, when you are happy and fulfilled, so will be the folks that love and care about you - and the others, well that doesn't really matter, they will find their way too eventually.

You may start this external environment change by just realizing what bothers you in your own little burg. Is your home organized and clean? Is your office, your car, your gym bag, your purse? Do you have a favorite place to sit and collect your thoughts that makes you feel good? Start here to correct what may be bothering you. Check each thing. Ask do I feel good or I feel bad when I think of this item. If it doesn't feel good, change it in some way to improve your feelings about it.

Now extend this to your yard, neighborhood, town or city, and country. Once you have looked that over and observed your feelings about each, you may need to just fantasize in the short run about what would be better. Make a vision board and dream a bit about what would a better situation actually look like. Once you have done this, now look again at your associations, jobs, friends, and commitments. How do they make you feel. Be honest with yourself. Positive change can be a reality only if you become aware that things you like and don't like and the things you want to improve or remove.

Sometimes it helps to just identify it all in writing. Write a letter to yourself about it all, they way you see it today and what you would like to see in the future. Put this letter in an envelope and open it next year for a pleasant surprise. Awareness or consciousness is like magic!

An ancient practice that many use to help with their surroundings is feng shui. I have personally found this to be fun, inspirational, and goal-oriented. There are many approaches to this eastern principal which can be utilized in all areas of your life. You can re-stage any environment you occupy to bring a different energy to that space. I have had my homes and work spaces decorated and configured with the help of a Feng Shui consultant and have always been fascinated by the results. I have friends who have done it to find or create healthy relationships, better health, better careers, wealth and prosperity and more. It is fun and interesting and creates change, again, even just subtle change can make a major difference.

So your health and happiness is really what this chapter is about. Boldly change whatever you must to find this for yourself. Everyone that matters will be glad you did!

ABOUT THE AUTHOR: *Donna LaBar*

 When author Donna LaBar shares her 30 years of study into nutritional healing, her eyes light up and her beauty defies her years. A lifetime resident of the rural Pennsyvania town of Tunkhannock, LaBar is sought after for healing information on cancer, diabetes, arthritis, weight loss, and more. Her gift? LaBar is a master of translating the healing power of an alkaline body into layman's terms. LaBar starts with the story of how her daughter healed from an adult form leukemia when she was a child.

LaBar receives calls for help nearly every week from individuals who do not know where else to turn. Her gentle guidance is recognized for its effectiveness, as shown in the stories she shares in her new book. She is self-taught in the field of medicinal properties of nutrition. Find out more about Donna's life work at www.DonnaLaBar.com.

Chapter 11

Manifesting a Life You Love... using Feng Shui

By Sybilla Lenz

The following information is written in a series of steps to help you remember an easy method for employing Feng Shui in your life to help you have a life that you love....

Simplify your life. There isn't much information out there that doesn't talk about the detrimental effects of too much clutter. So let's define clutter and the problem with clutter. It is defined as "a collection of things lying about in an untidy mess". One of the reasons that Feng Shui masters and teachers discuss moving things or eliminating clutter is to help change the energy of a space. Everything in our environment has a vibrational frequency and when we move things we help to change those vibrations and encourage chi flow in areas that have low or very little chi flow. "Chi" is the energy permeating everything in our environment and can either be slow, stagnant (shar-chi), or fast moving chi. It is ideal to have a nice meandering flow of chi in our environments. Sometimes moving items along with encouraging a faster chi movement is helpful for manifesting things you desire like a new home, better career, and even help in attracting a loving relationship. The following illustrates an example of manifesting and removing clutter.

I received a gift from my Uncle, a beautiful set of antique dishes that were over 100 years old. I loved the dishes but wondered where I would store them. I had a space I thought might work but first had to thoroughly clean the area. I then knew that I wanted and "intended" to have a beautiful buffet or break-front server to store the dishes in. I set the dishes on the floor in the space I created for the new buffet. I knew I would find or attract the perfect buffet because I used intention and created the space for it. Within three months I was approached by an antique dealer who knew that I wanted the perfect buffet server to house the dishes and she said she thought she found the perfect piece. It fit the space perfectly and was 100 years old in perfect condition just like the dishes! This happened in the early days of using Feng Shui principles for manifesting and I was delighted!

Consider spending some time going from room to

room and move items or piles of things you aren't needing or using to another space or room. Buy plastic storage bins if you feel you can't eliminate the items entirely and store them in a neat area in your basement or closet. Check that all of your closets are clean and organized. Eliminate clutter under beds and any other area that may have stacks of items that have not been moved in the last six months.

Chi loves to move along walls and floors in a meandering way. When it is unable to move it is stagnated or if it moves too fast it can be harsh and uncomfortable to the occupants in a space. What would you like to manifest or change? What area in your space has the most clutter? Take that area and completely clear it. Change, move, and simply the stuff in your space and watch your life change in magical ways.

Transform your environment using color. Sometimes when designing a room for change it is helpful to take out everything in the room you are changing and start with an empty palette. Take a good look at the color on the walls of the particular space you are changing. How do you feel about the color? If there are curtains, what color are they? Do you love them? These are important questions because how you feel about those questions dictate how your energy or chi is inside of you. When you transform your space, you transform your energy. Color is a great and simple way to enhance or change a room and has many messages or vibrations associated with it. For example, red is a high vibration color and can raise the blood pressure of people wearing the color. A red comforter that you sleep under may be the cause of some of the insomnia you could be experiencing. Having a red bedroom could be too energetic for some but having a red dining room might be the perfect color for aiding digestive fire.

Green is a "wood" element and can be associated with growth and balance. Blue is considered a "water" color and is also considered to be a color used for calming environments creating peace. Indigo is a deeper color of blue and can create a feeling of seren-ity and often used in settings to control anger. Violet or purple is warming and stimulating to the body.

Orange is also warming and energizing to wear and be surrounded in. When you are not sure what color to use, consider white. It embodies all the colors and can create a sense or feelings of clarity and purity.

Consider the vibrational message the color is sending you in your environment, especially in your bedroom where you spend one-third of your life. The color along with all the other elements should be very sup-portive, calming, and uplifting to your energy. Notice the shapes of things present in the rooms where you spend most of your time. Is there an overabundance of one element?

Once you have simplified and transformed the space

then consider giving away those things you no longer need or want in your space. Maybe someone else needs those things. Giving creates a wonderful opportunity for manifesting and attracting abundance in your life. It makes you feel good automatically raising your chi and it makes your environment feel spacious and energetically balanced too. Last but not least you are helping someone else in your giving and that is the best part of transformation!

Enhance and energize using the elements. Remember that everything is living and moving energy and vibration. Our home is a reflection of our life, so the best place to understand and enhance the energy is our home. How does your home feel? Connect with your home on sensory level, apply adjustments, and watch your life change. Start this practice by looking at the area surrounding your home.

In some schools of Feng Shui the front door is the most important door to examine for beneficial chi flow. This also happens to be the area of focus for enhancing your career opportunities. First and foremost make sure the chi can get to your front door easily. Examine your entrance by standing with your back to the front door and face out taking everything in view into consideration. Is there a tree blocking your view? Are you at the end of a street? Are there flowers in the front of your property, on, or at the door?

Is there anything obstructing the path to the door? Is

there dirt, debris, or overgrown plants or bushes? Is the front door freshly painted? How is the hardware on the door? Does it sparkle or is it tarnished? To encourage good chi flow to your front door into your life you may want to add fresh or potted flowers to the front door or on the door itself.

Remove any debris to the front door and thoroughly examine and encourage good and beneficial chi to your front door. This can aid you in your life and help enhance work and career opportunity.

Having negative or blocked chi at your front door can reduce your power and that can negatively impact how you feel as you strive to live purposeful especially in your chosen career or vocation.

Are there any structures facing or diagonal from your home that are sending negative energy in form of poison arrows? Is there an excess of electromagnetic frequencies coming into your home? An over concentration of EMF (electro-magnetic frequencies) can produce negative energy in the home and impact the occupants.

One way to enhance the energy in your home is to consider designing it with all the elements present in every room. Be especially attentive to those rooms where you spend the most time such as the family room or bedroom. The five elements are fire, earth, metal, water, and wood. One way to do this is to look at a predominant room and decide what element is represented in that room the most. Is it the wood element? Wood is represented by wood elements or the color green. Is there an overabundance of house plants? Although this can be lovely it can be over-powering to have only one or two elements present in the space. You want to balance an overabundance of this element by adding some fire to reduce its power, while adding some of the other elements in various shapes and colors with pillows and other decorative objects. It is possible to reverse the effects of a dull and lifeless space by enhancing the area with the shapes and colors of other elements.

Passion and power will come to the forefront now once you have moved, transformed , and energized your space. If you talk with anyone who is living their life on purpose and full of passion, they will tell you they love their work and their life. The great news is that it is entirely possible for you to feel that way too! When you live your life on purpose then your heart sings with joy, whether you are working or home enjoying your home.

Self Actualization is the master key to living a life you love. Last but not least this is one of the most important steps in manifesting. By experience I have found that I can simplify and de-clutter, transform or redesign my home, energize and intend until the cows come home but if I don't know what I am believing on the deepest level of my being about the intended desire I am trying to achieve it may not happen. I will give a little example to illustrate this.

My desire is to have a home that I love and feel warm and comfortable in. I also desire that for my family when they come home to visit. On one particular visit my daughter came home for the weekend with her family and I want her to have a "perfect" visit. I always try to have the rooms comfortable and clean and pleasant along with good foods. The week before they arrived we had adopted two little kittens before the visit and had to keep them inside in a closed room because one of them wasn't feeling well. Sometimes the "kitten smell" would come out of the room they were in, much to my dislike.

My daughter's husband is allergic to cats and I was concerned this might disrupt their comfort. I slept very little the night they were there and wondered where all the anxiety I was feeling was coming from. As I looked inside after they left for their journey home I realized how fearful I was that they might not be comfortable or come back because of the kitten. I also knew that was ridiculous because my daughter would not stay away because of a temporary situation like kittens posed. I knew it had to be more than that.

Even though I created a beautiful outward environment, I carried a belief that it is not good enough. I was fearful because of some deep subconscious beliefs creating the anxiety. I had made some choices in my youth with my young children that didn't always make them feel comfortable at home. I never forgave myself for some of my past and I carried that part of me every time I prepared my home for their visits.

I knew the answer was to forgive myself once and for all and hoped my family would now always feel comfort in my home. The very next day after I did some intention and prayerful release about a belief I was carrying, my daughter called to say that they had a lovely time and that she wished I would stop being so concerned when they were home because they loved being with me! I cleared myself of old negative beliefs ruining my peace and created a lovely home.

Self-actualized people know who they are completely, what they are intending, and are clear in that intention about their manifestation. When you follow the STEPS to manifest your dreams and desires and you feel you are doing all that you can do but still remain stuck, then dig deeper inside yourself for the answer....it is always there! We can create a beautiful space to live in and invite others to but our inner space may call out for attention too. When you clear and create a beautiful space inside and out your home your life will radiate with abundant chi. Feng Shui is a beautiful ancient philosophy and western tool to help you achieve a life you love. Pursue your passions and live a life of positive possibility!

ABOUT THE AUTHOR: *Sybilla Lenz*

 Sybilla Lenz, of Tunkhannock, PA, is a certified Feng Shui consultant in three schools of Feng Shui with over 12 years of experience in both practical applications and giving presentations and workshops. Sybilla attributes her own peace and harmony along with amazing and positive changes for others to the use of Feng Shui. Sybilla has also co-authored books titled Welcome Home and Designing Hospitals of the Future. "I've always wanted to share my own personal story to help others in their quest for living their best life possible. Being a part of this book has allowed me to reach thousands of people – just like me – who are perhaps searching for ways to increase abundance in their lives. I hope others will learn from my experiences and achieve their goals that much faster," says Sybilla.

You can learn more about Sybilla on her website:
www.positivelivingfengshui.com

Chapter 12

The Solopreneur Inner Makeover:

The Secret Ingredient Successful Solopreneurs Use to Reach Six Figures With Ease And Live a Balanced, Joyful Life

By Heather Finley, Ph.D.

I'm honored you have chosen to discover what this inner makeover is all about. Here are a few questions to ask yourself as you begin this chapter...

Have you ever felt exhausted because you are juggling too many balls in the air at an incredibly hectic pace?

Have you been disappointed that, despite your AMAZING juggling feat, business profits are lagging?

Do you simply have too many balls to juggle, and feel overwhelmed as they continue to drop all around you?

Do you realize that while you have been so focused on juggling, your life is passing by too quickly?!

If you answered yes to any of these questions, this chapter was written specifically for you!

Ask me how I knew you might say "yes" to at least one of those questions? As a recovering juggler, I too have experienced all of the above at one time or another. Several years ago, I realized I was trying to do too much, for too little money, at too great a LIFESTYLE COST. So I began my own inner makeover to transform my experience from one of being overworked, overwhelmed, and underpaid to one of working and living in a way that is peaceful, prosperous, and joyful.

That means I am able to spend much more time with my son during his pre-school years and beyond. It means I can prioritize quality time with my life partner and incorporate my Zumba dance addiction into my work week. And it means I am on the path to financial freedom.

The key to making these changes existed between my ears the entire time I was juggling and feeling the pain of a being a stressed out, underpaid solopreneur! Now if I was able to make those inner changes, you can too. I didn't do it alone, mind you. I had coaches, mentors, and colleagues to guide me into an entirely new way of thinking.

Inner Makeover

As psychologist-turned-success coach, I realized that other solopreneurs could benefit from this same transformation.

I am certainly not the first to teach others how to use the power of our minds to develop a success attitude and powerful inner game. Attention to our inner experiences and their outer manifestations is what the field of psychology is ALL about. But most business schools and business owners pay little attention to understanding how the "inner game" works.

So I'm bridging the gap between psychology and business to teach a time-tested method that will improve the inner landscape of solopreneurs so that the results you are aiming for seem to manifest in ways that don't even feel like hard work! Solopreneurs who allow an inner makeover find their business profits begin to skyrocket, their time at work at least 43% more productive, and their free time plentiful to spend on their life priorities, such as family, health, and fun. Far beyond profit, the balance of work and life brings its own sweet rewards.

This inner makeover is a proven method that combines psychological principles; my own observations from over 20 years of helping my clients become more confident, positive, productive, and happy; self-study of topics I didn't learn in school (such as the Law of Attraction, business fundamentals, and prosperity thinking); AND life and business lessons learned along the way. The inner makeover is so powerful, that after these inner changes occur, my clients are easily able to use the remaining success strategies to transform their businesses and lives from being stressed, unhappy, and broke to being confident, successful and balanced. I have had clients leave toxic relationships, eliminate money worries, get promoted, spend 10 fewer hours at work each week, and begin living joyful, balanced lives.

Before you begin your inner makeover, take a moment and think about any successful person in business, sports, music, or any other field. Oprah Winfrey. Donald Trump. Beyonce. Roger Federer. What do they all have in common? Yes, they all have a success mindset.

You might be saying, "Sure, that makes sense, Heather. How do I get a success mindset?" Good question. You can't buy one. You can't swap brains unless you're doing some crazy Frankenstein experiment! The way you get a success mindset is simple, but not necessarily easy. A success mindset consists of voices inside your head. I call them "Success Scripts." These scripts can lift you up to the highest heights. They speak from a place of confidence and possibility-thinking. They encourage persistence. They hold an indisputable belief that your goals will be achieved. They support getting back up after a fall. They congratulate for a job well done and celebrate milestones along the way.

Undermining Scripts

Success scripts have to be constantly rehearsed to feed and support your accomplishments. Because as you can imagine, scripts also have the power to destroy you: directly or in more subtle ways. Scripts represent the inner dialogue we have in our minds. And just as the water cooler dialogue changes as people observe differences in the weather, so our inner dialogue changes as we observe our own external world. Depending on how well-developed our success scripts are, that inner dialogue can undermine us as we experience challenges in our business and personal lives.

Many solopreneurs don't succumb to the complete destruction I referenced before, but are much more familiar with the subtle ways that undermining scripts conjure up words such as "failure" and "defeat." When you feel like you are banging your head against the same brick wall or spinning your wheels, pay attention to your inner scripts. They are not coming from a success mindset.

Subtle ways the scripts undermine your success is when they sound something like this: "No matter what I do, I just can't win." Or "I can't catch a lucky break." Unfortunately, I have had clients whose negative scripts were so well-entrenched, that they were on the loudspeaker for most situations they found themselves in. When those negative scripts are so entrenched, they actually become the filter through which you see the world and your experiences. So the quality of that filter, the nature of your scripts, makes all the difference.

Imagine how a solopreneur with any of the undermining scripts above would behave when he or she made a sales presentation to 50 people but didn't make one sale. The scripts would get louder and louder, reinforcing the point with every rejection until finally, she gives up, believing those scripts to be "the truth." Enter the agony of defeat. I have seen this time and time again throughout my career when I begin with clients. Their undermining scripts have the familiarity one would have with a childhood nursery rhyme. "It's raining, I'm boring, my old ideas deploring… Business dread inside my head, I couldn't get up in the morning!"

Undermining scripts can also negatively impact your business profits because of what the scripts say about money and wealth. I have worked with people who did not see their own value, such as a pet sitter named Paula who was afraid to raise her rates, or healing professionals who were reluctant to charge a cancellation fee to clients who didn't show up for their appointments. With repetition, confidence begins to erode. And in order to make a profit or sometimes to just break even, they end up working long, hard hours and begin to question if their business is even worth the effort. It all stems from a combination of low self-confidence, low self-worth, potentially combined with unhealthy attitudes about money and wealth...all of which emerge from and are reinforced by undermining scripts.

Another common way these scripts can be counter-productive has to do with what the scripts say about time and getting things done. As a solopreneur, you wear so many hats that a full day's work whizzes by. Before you know it, the month, the quarter, and the year has come and gone. AND you probably feel exhausted because you have been putting out fires and plodding through the drudgery that your business requires. Usually, the undermining scripts that keep this hamster spinning around and around (and around!) on that wheel to nowhere sound something like:

"I'm the only one who can do this work." Or "I can't afford to hire anyone else." Or "Someday, I'll have time to create a system to be more productive and profitable in my business." Or "I have no time or energy for my family." These scripts, if repeated often enough, become truth. And if that is your truth, not much will change outwardly in your business and you will continue to feel trapped as you spin around and around in that hamster wheel.

As you can imagine, these undermining scripts, if left

to their own devices, will prevent you from having a successful, profitable business and a balanced life. In fact, they are likely the main roadblocks that are currently preventing you from attaining true prosperity … where you are paid handsomely to do the work you love and you have plenty of time to spend with your family, be healthy, and live a life that YOU design!

Scripting Your Way to Success

The GREAT news is that you currently have everything you need to reach six figures or whatever your profit target is, to work productively and efficiently, and to live a fulfilling and fun life. And it all lies in the six inches between your ears. Our minds are so incredibly powerful…You don't have to be a psychologist to know that! AND, like anything with great power, you must fully understand the ins and outs of operating it. Take a moment to think about one of your major accomplishments. What were the success scripts inside your head that propelled you toward achieving that goal? What were the undermining scripts that tried to get in your way? And how did you overcome them? If those undermining scripts were the loudest and most frequent, do you think you would have attained that accomplishment? Probably not! Notice that your skills would have been no different.

Your level of success is not about how much you know or how many skills you have. They help, certainly, but without the secret ingredient of a success mindset, you wouldn't have achieved that accomplishment. Or if you did, it probably took A LOT longer with much more struggle than you needed to have.

Believe me, I am not suggesting that all you have to do is think positively and wish for different results and they will magically appear. But I AM talking about creating a new external reality by beginning with a new and improved internal reality. And when you start from within, the outer results you achieve often do feel like magic.

Three Steps to an Inner Makeover

Here's the inner makeover method I promised at the beginning of the chapter. Take these three simple steps and your business and life will transform.

Step One: Identify All Your Undermining Scripts. Become fully aware of the scripts that are currently undermining your success. Start with the symptoms in your external world and work backwards to identify the underlying beliefs that are contributing to those symptoms. For example, if you are disorganized and missing deadlines, what is the thought behind that symptom? Is it, "I can't afford to hire help." Or "I just don't have time to get organized." Whatever it is, and there may be more than one, list them all on a piece of paper.

Step Two: Create A Success Script To Replace Each

Undermining Script. On a blank piece of paper, create a list of success scripts to replace each script identified in Step One. Think of the undermining scripts as weeds. If you don't attend to that one weed in the yard, it will undoubtedly spread. To get rid of weeds, all of them have to be removed. You'll find that undermining scripts may "grow back," but as you strengthen your mindset with success scripts, it will be much easier to pluck out any weed seedling before it takes hold. To challenge the undermining scripts listed in step one, replacement success scripts could be "Hiring help will enable me to get organized, provide better service, and keep my customers happy." Or "I am getting more organized each day, and each missed deadline is an opportunity to improve my systems."

Step Three: Rehearse Your Success Scripts. Review your list of success scripts and rehearse them daily. Several times a day would be ideal. One simple strategy to ensure you rehearse them is to create three daily recurring appointments on your computer or smart phone. In the "notes" section, list your success scripts. Then set an alert and whenever it goes off, take a couple minutes to rehearse your scripts.

Success Scripts Manifest Outer Victories

After replacing those invasive, weed-like scripts with success scripts, you will harness a mega-watt power that will propel you toward achieving your desired goals. Sometimes, you won't even feel like you're making an effort because it just happens. That's when the Law of Attraction is at work and it can feel like magic. At other times, you will just have to practice new behaviors. Although initially uncomfortable, like when you start wearing a new pair of shoes, as you repeat these new scripts and behaviors, they will soon become familiar and comfortable, and those shoes will become your favorite pair!

After completing the three-step method above, you can follow these additional steps to gain clarity about your next actions so you can manifest those victories!

Step Four: Match Actions With Each Success Script. To the right of each success script, generate two to three action steps that are consistent with the script. In our running example, you might list "Research virtual assistants, create list of tasks I can outsource or delegate, and interview three possible sub-contractors." Or "File one pile of papers before leaving the office each day, create a to-do list for the next day, create a checklist to ensure I meet project deadlines."

Step Five: Perform Success Actions. Now, it's clear what you need to do to make your internal success scripts an external reality. This step is all about TAKING ACTION. As your success scripts become familiar and comfortable, the action steps will naturally follow. This reminds me of a powerful memory I have of a fellow coach who I would see at our quarterly trainings. He had been overweight for a long time; morbidly obese, in fact. Then at one of the training sessions, a man who looked a bit familiar stood up and began telling his story. It was this same man, but about half the size he used to be. He told us that he started losing weight when he started thinking like a thin person. When he went to a restaurant, he thought, "A thin person doesn't eat French fries and a burger. A thin person eats lots of vegetables and avoids fried food." And so he would order a salad and chicken breast. Perhaps this sounds obvious, but I thought it was profound. He didn't start losing weight until he changed his inner scripts. And then the behaviors easily followed. The same will happen for you.

This natural flow from inner success scripts to outer victories is where the EASE comes in. For a moment, just think about what happens when you drive home every day. You know exactly where you are going. You have every confidence in the world that you will arrive there. If a road is blocked for construction, you know how to take a detour and still arrive at your destination without letting it stop you. Most of the time, you actually get there without even having to think about it.

Driving home is an excellent analogy for how an inner makeover is the starting place that enables you to move toward your goals with confidence and laser-like focus. When you have this secret ingredient and know how to use it, you feel as certain about achieving your business goals as you do driving home. You

KNOW you will get there. You know the route you need to take. You know how to handle potential road-blocks. And most of the time, you experience ease as you move along the path. AND you always arrive at your destination.

The key to EASILY and QUICKLY attaining the results you are aiming for is inner scripting. Success scripts will propel you toward what you most want in your business and life. With your newly enhanced success mindset, you will feel like you just changed directions on a swift river and are no longer struggling to move forward against the current because you are now rowing downstream with the flow that seems to carry you and support your every stroke.

Business Makeover

This secret ingredient of having an unstoppable suc-cess mindset lives inside an 8-step business success formula that I created specifically to help solopreneurs achieve maximum profits, increase productivity, and live a lifestyle that is based on your top priorities: family, health, prosperity, and fun to name a few.
Imagine what it would be like to have more direc-tion and focus; to accomplish more without putting in extra hours; to have more time to spend with your family and do the things that you enjoy; to have the confidence to go after your ideal clients; to have an attitude that creates opportunities and directs your professional and personal decisions; and to have

a greater sense of inner peace. These are the exact words my past clients have used to describe what they attained after they had a business makeover using the elements in this 8-step success formula.

If you're like most solopreneurs, you started your business to make a great living doing the work you love, to have autonomy and freedom, and to design your life based on your priorities and values. I have a proven 8-step system designed to help you do just that. It not only goes into much more depth to generate (and maintain) the success mindset I've introduced you to in this chapter, but also gives you the seven other key ingredients you absolutely need to maximize your business profits and to be one of those business owners who leads a low-stress and balanced life. Six-figure solopreneurs working a part-time schedule and loving their lives use these same eight steps.

As Buddha said so eloquently, "What we are today comes from our thoughts of yesterday, and our present thoughts build our life of tomorrow: Our life is the creation of our mind." If you are not fully satisfied with where you are in your business or your personal life today, you have the power to change it. It starts with a Success Mindset. It is the foundational, secret ingredient. I would love the opportunity to share with you in more depth the seven remaining ingredients that build upon that foundation and give you everything you need to create the business and life you want.

Are you ready for a business makeover that can help you dramatically boost your income without working longer hours so you have plenty of time and money for family, health, and fun?

I've put together a FREE training to provide you with a business makeover that can quickly transform your business to one with outrageous productivity and profits and your life to one that doesn't revolve around work. A life with plenty of MONEY AND TIME to live the balanced, joyful life you have been desperately craving.

Simply go to **www.GetMyBusinessMakeover.com** and enroll at zero cost while I'm still offering this training for free.

You have the power to raise your business to the next level. And this business makeover will give you the entire roadmap, explaining just how to do it. The universe rewards action. Your reward is waiting…

As always, to your success and balance!
Heather

ABOUT THE AUTHOR: *Heather Finley, Ph.D.*

 I am fiercely committed to guiding solopreneurs and mompreneurs to eliminate the overwhelm of wearing too many hats, working too many hours, and suffering from sluggish business profits, so they can experience the true freedom that comes from a booming business and plenty of free time to enjoy family and live a truly joyful and balanced life.

If you are looking for a proven professional who can guide you to eradicate the invisible inner blocks that are standing in your way, to break through your financial ceiling, and to stop missing out on life because you're logging way too many hours at work, you've come to the right place.

With over 20 years of experience working with amazing clients who have had similar concerns, I have facilitated some remarkable success. My mission is to redefine what it means to be a successful business owner and to provide a time-tested system that paves the way for entrepreneurs to have wildly successful businesses and lifestyles that reflect their values and priorities. This "new entrepreneur" is making the world a better place because of what their businesses provide, how they are living their lives, and the ripple effect they create. My vision is to help make the world a better place one new entrepreneur at a time.

My path to become a success coach who insists that our inner game is the secret ingredient to attaining all that our hearts desire became clear at an early age. As a 10-year-old, when most of my friends were reading comic books, I was reading about ESP (Extrasensory Perception) and was enthralled with the power of our minds and the endless possibilities. While taking Psychology 101 in my first year of college, it became crystal clear that I wanted to become a psychologist, and the fascination continues still!

What lights me up about this work is knowing that within every person is the potential to share their unique gifts with the world and to live a joyful and fulfilling life. I get to facilitate my clients' changes from the inside out, improving their inner game and practical outer world strategies. It is truly rewarding to admire the unique butterfly that emerges from that transformation.

What sets me apart from other business coaches is the depth I bring as a veteran psychologist who understands how to tap into underlying motivation, the secrets to making lasting changes, and techniques to get past the internal and external blocks that interfere with progress. I have combined psychology expertise, business best practices, prosperity thinking, and the Law of Attraction to create an 8-step success formula designed specifically for solopreneurs and mompreneurs (it works for dadpreneurs too!).

Over the years, my expertise has been honored with remarkable and notable accolades, including graduating Cum Laude from the University of Notre Dame, earning a doctorate in counseling psychology before the age of 30, filling a full-time private practice within a year of being fresh out of graduate school, and more recently, developing an 8-step success formula specifically for solopreneurs.

My perspectives have been shared on local radio and television, workshops and seminars, and as a main speaker at regional and national conferences. Some of my experiences might surprise and delight you. First of all, I too am a solopreneur and mompreneur, with an amazing young son. I am so grateful I can attend his pre-school activities and spend more time with him during my reduced-hour work week. I also have developed multiple streams of income. After being a landlady for a handful of years, I switched to private lending and now enjoy a steady stream of passive income to quickly and easily build wealth.

My top values and priorities are health, family, balance, freedom, and respect. In addition to seeing clients, my work week is currently a delightful blend of spending time with my son and life partner, dancing Zumba-style, arranging music and singing in a guitar-piano duo (Voices2), brushing the rust off my tennis game, and spending as much time as possible outdoors.

I feel at least 10 years younger than I am — which I attribute to being creative and engaged in a rich life of variety and growth. I have several exciting possibilities for success coaching that are percolating and coming down the pike, including virtual VIP Days, Quarterly Live VIP Days, and Business Makeover Retreats in Costa Rica or some other exotic location. Life is good!

As always…To Your Success and Balance…
Heather Finley, Ph.D.
Heather@GetMyBusinessMakeover.com
www.MyInnerSolutions.com

Chapter 13

How to Manifest a Millionairess Life with No Money

By Stacia Loo

I am currently the marketing director for Thach Real Estate Group, a Seattle-based real estate company and it is really a dream job that I manifested for myself. Many people ask me how I manifested the absolutely perfect job for me.

Before I share with you how I manifested my dream job, let me tell you a little bit about me. I grew up in the most beautiful place in the world, some call it paradise: Honolulu, Hawaii. I was born and raised on the island of Oahu and had a great childhood. I was the only child for many years and I was given almost everything I wanted as a kid. I was able to participate in all types of activities, basketball, ballet,

karate, dance classes, swimming lessons and more...
Life was great!

Until my parents divorced, then I became a child of a
broken home. My mom became a single mother and
raised me the best that she knew how. She ended
up re-marrying and having my brother and sister.
More changes into the family dynamics but long story
short, I become a big sister with a 12-year difference
in between my siblings. Being the oldest, I took on
the role of wanting to help and take care of everyone.
Money soon became very tight and my mom would
say to me things like "Don't you get it! We don't have
enough money!!".

Words are so powerful! Did you grow up around the
same words such as: money doesn't grow on trees,
rich people are snobs, you have to have money to
make money or how about **"money is the root of all
evil"?**

Did you believe in those sayings? I did...

I was told by my grandfather you should get good
grades, go to school, work with computers and
"WORK HARD" for your money.

My father was a hard worker, and he still is today.
There is nothing wrong with people who work hard.
I am still a hard worker. I just learned that I want
to work smarter, not harder. I saw my father work

so much I hardly saw the guy. All of the photos of my birthday parties I would see my dad in his work clothes just getting off of work. He inspired me I guess. Unconsciously, I ended up taking on the same work ethic.

The minute I could, I enrolled in a work program when I was 15. My senior year in high school I had two jobs. One I worked Monday to Friday, the other I worked 10 hours Saturday and Sunday. I thought that is the way it worked. I would literally count how much money I wanted to make by the number of hours I needed to work. If they were giving any over-time I would take it. I worked myself so much during college I didn't see any other way. I went to school for 20 hours a week and worked 60 hours a week.

Then I found myself pregnant and a single mom at 19, and I had to start slowing down. I had to pay a babysitter to watch my son while I continued to work and found out quick that I was paying the babysitter with one check and paying the rent with the other check. I had no time, no money, and hated my life.

I was missing out on my son's firsts… and too tired to enjoy my time with him. I couldn't qualify for any government assistance since I worked too much. I couldn't qualify for many grants to finish school. But I was determined…

Plus I really didn't want any government assistance

because I am stubborn and I wanted to say I did it on my own. I did end up finishing school and pushing through. I was very proud of myself that I finished school, when statistics show that the chances of a single mom finishing school is very rare.

After finishing school I did get a job and was promoted but, about 1 year later I was laid off. Now I was $30,000 in debt for school with a degree that competitively would only grant me a job making $10 an hour. I felt like I had to start over again.

I don't say this to make you feel sorry for me. I am also not saying college was a waste of time. This was the best thing that ever happened to me.

It was just the price I paid to learn the biggest LESSON of my life…

I chose to step away and re-examine what is next in my life. I went to stay with relatives and that is where my aunt and uncle shared with me a game called "Cash Flow 101" by Robert Kiyosaki, the author of Rich Dad, Poor Dad. This was the tipping point that turned it all around for me. It was the first time I heard the concept of working hours for dollars verses passive income.

Who knew that you could work one time and have money coming in every month like clockwork?
I was working as a customer care representative

taking inbound and outbound calls. I had been in that industry right out of high school and got really good at it. After nine years in the industry I got very burnt out and hated being stuck to a cubicle answering phone calls from angry customers. I had no idea how life could be anything different, I kept wishing that my job would lay me off.

Guess what I manifested? I got laid off! Being laid off was the best thing that ever happened to me. This was my chance to figure out what I really wanted to do with my life. I wanted to be laid off but I was also scared, what am I going to do?

I was introduced to my first entrepreneurial venture in 2007. I was introduced to more books like "The Secret". I started studying marketing, self-development, and went to hear all of the gurus share their knowledge about how an ordinary person can make significant changes in their life by the way we think.

Learning these new tools, I knew there had to be a better way. At the end of 2008, I came to terms with my first failed business. I ended up moving back to Seattle to live with my mother. This was a low point in my life and I had no idea where my next dollar was going to come from.

What I had learned though is that I can be very resource, somehow and someway I always made it work. Though I still had negative people in my life that would tell me, when are you going to get a **"Real Job"**.

So I started hanging out with people who were just like me. I found a group of like minded people and had like minded people introduce me to more amazing people every day. I would just listen to people and find out what is important to them what people were working on and would genuinely see how I can contribute to them.

One day I went out to a fundraising event with a few friends to get out and mingle. I usually keep my camera with me at all times and saw the opportunity to videotape a great speaker Thach Nguyen, who is the CEO of Thach Real Estate Group. Of course I whipped out my camera and started filming. It has really been a second nature habit that I do. Anyone that knows me I am the first one to whip out the camera at any opportunity.

I went home posted it to Facebook and tagged him in the video. If you don't know what tagging is, basically it is a way to show who is in your photo or video and the person you tag gets notified they have been tagged in a photo or video. **I did this truly out of contribution, not really knowing what would happen. I just thought it was cool and posted it.**

A few days later get a phone call from him and he said **"how did you do that?"** I was shocked! I had no idea he was looking for an assistant to get him started in the world of social media to grow his business. We went on and chatted about my passion for real estate as an investor, as an entrepreneur and my love for connecting with people. We set an appointment for a formal in-person interview a week later. In the mean time, I went on to his blog and listened to a coaching call that he recorded with his coach on finding the perfect assistant. I took notes and what he was look-ing for and I had this feeling of definite purpose that the person he was describing as his perfect assistant was me!

This could not be better timing. Well, it could have been, but everything happens for a reason. Like I was saying earlier I had no clue when my next dollar was coming from. On the day of my job interview, I was jobless. I had no sales coming in from miscellaneous sales jobs I had been connected with. Bills were piling up, my car payment was past due two months and the next thing you know my car was missing. I thought my car was stolen, but indeed it was the REPO-man. I had to dig up the funds to get it out of repo yard, get a ride 40 miles away to pick up my car and go to this interview.

My friend had told me to ask my future millionaire boss for money up front to get me out of this situation. I said "no way". I could not do that… I knew I had to go in there with a positive energy, let go of the drama. I just wanted to focus on what I could contribute to the millionaire and his wife. I felt really good about the interview and then I received a call and got hired right away. We agreed on a six-month trial period which turned into three years and is still going strong.

I just manifested a position working with a "Millionaire". What an opportunity! That is how "The Millionairess in Training" was born.
I realized I wanted to share this journey with the world and share with others what I am learning working with a millionaire.

What is a Millionairess in Training?

A woman who is training to be a millionaire.

A person who studies the habits of achievers and the successful.

A person who is developing their skills and mindset to live their life by design.

A person who declares to be and do what ordinary people won't, to make dreams into reality.

The question you might be asking is *"OK, how do you become a Millionairess in Training?"*

11 Ways to Become a "Millionairess in Training"

1. Leaders are Readers. I started devouring books. I

read/listened to hundreds of books. If you want to be better at anything someone has written a book about.

2. Be Curious. I started to learn how to ask questions. Be an interviewer. Come from a place of curiosity in others. Find out how the successful went from where they were to where they are now. That is why I started my blog, TheMillionairessinTraining.com to interview people I am inspired by. I have learned so much by these interviews and then at the same time share them with you, the world.

3. Be Clear On What You Want. When you are clear on what you want, you will never feel overwhelmed. You will be so focused on what you want that others shiny objects will not get in your way. When you are clear it will make it easier to say "No" to things that are not aligned with you. When you are clear you will also attract exactly what you want when you are clear.

4. Network with People of Affluence and Influence. When you surround yourself with people that you want to be more like it literally starts to rub off on you. I was told "Your Network is Your Net worth" and If You Want to Soar with Eagles, Don't Hang Out with Turkeys. If you are not clear on what you want people in your sphere of affluence can help you be a sounding board to help you get clear on your focus.

5. Have a burning desire. I know that when I set my sights on something and have no doubts, that is when things come to me. I have won several things at various raffle drawings and it might sound weird but I always knew right before they called my name I was going to win.

"Desire is the starting point of all achievement, not a hope, not a wish, but a keen pulsating desire which transcends everything." —Napoleon Hill

6. Contribution. "You will get all you want in life, if you help enough other people get what they want." - Zig Ziglar. I have lived by this saying all my life and then the millionaire I work for today wrote a book about the Law of Contribution, it is called The Gift - A Revolution in Networking Mastery.

7. Resourcefulness. Be creative in stressful or difficult situations. I had a great grandfather at the time that was very ill. He had shared with my aunt that all he wanted to was to see his boy, my son Makaya. I had no extra money to send my son from Seattle, Washington to Honolulu during a peak season which cost about $700 dollars the very next day. My mom and I had an undoubting feeling that no matter what, not sure how, but that I would find the money. I went into resource mode and started calling people close to me for ideas and support. Some wished they had the money to give to me and some had great ideas. We were down to a few more hours and my mom was determined to live the next morning. My boyfriend checked my mail and a check had arrived that I was sure it was not supposed to arrive for another week. I manifested the money again within a few hours, having an unshakeable faith my son was going to get on a plane to Hawaii the next day.

8. Gratitude. There has been many times in my life where I was flat broke. Had no idea where my next dollar would be coming from and somehow money would drop from the sky. I have to share with you a time when I had no idea how we were going to pay our rent. The rent was overdue, I had to walk my son to school because my car broke down. I took the time to go to the nearest beach to release and meditate. I went and listened to the ocean and just be thankful and appreciative for what I had in front of me. As I walked back to my apartment I get a phone call that flashed unknown caller. I don't know about you but I never answer unknown calls. If you were as broke as I was you probably wouldn't either, I was afraid it would be a creditor. I had a feeling just answer it anyways, it happened to be an insurance company calling to find out where to send me $3800 to settle an accident that happened to me about 3 years prior. I believe that was evidence that I can manifest change in a matter of minutes.

9. Be Coachable. I was willing to let go of my past and learn what the successful people are doing. I asked for feedback. I continue to ask for coaching and be open to masterminding with others.

10. Find a Mentor. When I interview people I look to my experts as mentors. If you want to learn how to do anything why not ask people who have already done it. You can find out a lot from people who already failed a 1,000 times to become the experts they are today. If you can't meet or find a mentor in person there are tons of people you can read about. Back to lesson one, leaders are readers.

11. Take Massive Action. Knowledge is power only if you take massive action. Don't wait for the right timing, the right weather, the right whatever to show up. Take action, if you fail you will get back up. Every time you fall you will find a new way. The difference between the millionaire and those who are not yet is that we haven't failed enough. Sitting around, waiting to get ready, waiting for something magical to happen good luck.

So, take action in spite of fear.

You can be a Millionairess with No Money.

I have used these tips to manifest trips, airfare, vacations, hotels, and money. I also manifested a home, money, jobs, and the love of my life. If you can dream it, you can have it all. I really believe you can be a Millionairess with No Money.

I ask people all the time…

"How would you feel if you had a Million Dollars?"

"What would you do if you had a Million Dollars?"

"What would you like to have if you had a Million Dollars?"

Whatever the answer is you can have it NOW. Hold on to the emotion of having it already. It might be hard to feel something before it happens. But just pretend. Soon you will be expecting more and nothing less. Soon you will have things happen in your life that seems like it literally happened out of thin air.

Just being a part of this book was a miracle. I had written down that I wanted to write a book a long time ago and I didn't put much energy into it. When the time was right the opportunity came in a way that I never thought of a collaboration book. Talk about something even better.

I am not a Millionairess yet but I certainly feel like one. I have the same opportunities as a millionaire. I have created a support system of resources. I can have anything I set my sights on. Some things may not come to me as fast as being a true millionaire, but it is all in the works. I am very appreciative of everything I have now and very eager for more...

I hope this inspires you to become a Millionairess in Training Today!

ABOUT THE AUTHOR: *Stacia Loo*

Stacia discovered the Millionairess in Training after she landed a position working for a real estate millionaire in Seattle, WA. Her mission, the Millionairess in Training, was born. If you want to become anything in life, interview and duplicate what others that have already done it. Her goal is to achieve balance and simplicity in these areas by studying mentors, implementing their habits/actions and contributing to the lives of others. Join me at www.TheMillionairessinTraining.com and have a Millionairess Day!

Chapter 14

Change and the Hero's Journey

By Mike and Donna Stott

To be willing to change is the start of a heroic endeavor. It's about leaving the comfortable (or the uncomfortable) status quo and taking a chance on the mysteries that are possible. Just by holding and reading this book, you are showing that you are willing to do something extraordinary... to change something significant in your life. It might be your job, financial situation, weight, health, dietary or exercise habits or thousands of other possibilities.

Make no mistake, "being willing" is your first step on the Hero's Journey that will call upon your deeper self, which is part of your core and includes your natural gifts and talents.

Joseph Campbell describes the classic pattern of a

Hero's story in his book "A Hero with a Thousand Faces." In Campbell's work there are many steps or stages, and each story may include all or just a few. We'll go through four basic steps in a simple version of a hero's story. In our coaching work we use a Four Step model called Look; See; Tell the Truth; and take Authentic Action. These steps fit well in the four simplified steps of the journey.

Step One

Step One is recognizing that something needs to change in your ordinary world. It may be as strong as a "calling" or can be just a gentle nudge that keeps showing up... but there must be some acknowledgement by YOU of a need for action. And like every journey that every hero takes, it won't seem easy... nor will it be. The Hero's Journey always involves the expenditure of energy, courage, and growth. This is often referred to as the "Call to Adventure". In our coaching work we call this Looking... turning your attention toward something of importance.

Step Two

Step Two is a conscious acceptance or rejection of this call. With many journey callings, the answer may be a resounding NO, again and again, before a final YES that moves us forward. When we say "Yes" we are ready to start down what Campbell called the "Road of Trials". Hard work, challenge and set-backs appear on this road and it is a time of deep reflection. We call this step Seeing - looking more completely. As when you "look" at a magic eye picture and after shifting your focus, really "seeing" the picture that was there all the time - hidden from your view initially and then appearing, almost like magic.

Step Three

Step Three in the journey is where the Hero finally sees clearly and a path is laid before them. In this step, the hero must decide if he or she is on this journey alone, or if they will accept assistance. A mentor appears that will assist in helping the Hero to observe during this part of the journey. Until we can observe, we can't truly see clearly because we are not seeing it... we are being it. Another moment of decision occurs when deciding to turn back (I see... but I don't want to) or move forward during this step. We call this part of the Journey Telling the Truth in our coaching and it must be done before truly moving to the next step.

Step Four

Step Four is crossing the threshold from seeing to actions that are effective. Taking effective or authentic action leads to the discovery of important knowledge, a clearing of sludge in your life, a meaningful goal reached... in some way it is fulfillment of the Journey's intentions. In our coaching, we call this part Taking Authentic Action.

All this sounds like a movie plot and indeed, most every book, movie or story you've experienced follows the Hero's Journey… as well as the many stories within our lives. Manifesting change in a meaningful, conscious way means recognizing your part in the story as the Hero. Not just an "extra" in your movie… but the star of your story.

A Real Life Hero's Journey

We own a business coaching, consulting, and training company called Your Coaching Matters, and a true-life Hero's Journey story may help you see how this unfolds in real life. One of our long-term real estate agent clients set a goal to make an additional $58,000 a year in income. We ran the numbers with his average commission on sales, and this translated to needing an additional 12 closings a year. This already successful agent was getting a majority of current business from referrals and repeat business, but was at a plateau earning a little over $100,000 a year. Business expenses and lifestyle changes had him falling behind on credit card payments, car expenses, and home payments. This client recognized that something needed to change, Step One on the Journey.

We discussed in depth his desire to make the additional money and determined that he wanted this for inspiring and fulfilling reasons. This money would allow him to get out of debt, fund his child's college account, and start a retirement fund. All of these goals supported his primary Life's Intentions of being financially successful and being a loving parent.

This client developed a plan of action, which included adding lead generation in the form of contacting and scheduling visits with For-Sale-by-Owners (FSBOs) to offer assistance. However, after three weeks, the results were no new lead generation or FSBO visits were accomplished.

When we asked the client what was holding him back he responded "Every time I sit down to make the contacts, I come up with something else to do: check my email, handle another call, go to a meeting, and even do the laundry... anything but what I said I would do". The client went on further to say "and besides, FSBOs don't want me to bug them, and there are lots of other agents calling them, and they are all stubborn, unreasonable and mean anyway." Wow - No wonder the contacts weren't getting made! The Road of Trials was imagined so horribly and the distractions on the side of the road had become far more interesting than the goal. Note that this is normal on the Journey and remember, part of that Step Two is making a decision to accept or reject the call.

If we go back to the Hero's Journey, you'll see our client was someone who saw the need for change and heard a calling he longed for as a powerful Life's Intention... and created a vision of how to get to his goal. He thought he had decided to accept the challenge... and then stumbled. The client did not cross the threshold and take action.

How to Clear the Internal Chatter That Stops Us

In our coaching training through the Academy for Coaching Excellence (ACE), an approved Coaching accreditation school with the International Coaching Federation (ICF), we have learned useful tools for overcoming the internal chatter exhibited by our client. This chatter often keeps someone from taking the steps needed to change, so let's take a moment to look at one tool called The Playing Field.

Picture a typical football or soccer field with a midfield line we'll call "the border". The Upper half of the field we'll call "Physical Reality" and the Lower half of the field we'll call "Visionary Reality". When we play in the lower half of the field, goals and dream are easy to create, there's no cost or energy expended in visioning owning a nicer house, or having fully funded college accounts, or being debt free. It is light and airy and the possibilities are unlimited!

When we set goals in Physical Reality, though, there's a density there that requires the expenditure of energy (in the form of time, creativity, money, physical vitality, relationships, and/or enjoyment) to reach that goal. For our client, reaching the goal of paying off debts and funding college and retirement accounts required that he take the time to find prospects in his area, get creative with what he was going to say, be in an "of service" mindset offering value, go meet with them, provide them with information and ideas, and finally follow-through to earn their trust and business. All the while being positive and pleasant, and recognizing that he would need to do this 360 or more times to make the additional 12 sales he wanted to make. Whew! A long Step Two "road of trials" to get to that goal, isn't it? Can you feel the density and energy needed in all that work? It's no wonder that his internal chatter, which we call Monkey Mind, had a lot to say. The Monkey is loudest at the Border when we are JUST about to step into doing something big.

Even though our client had made nearly 200 career sales and had scores of testimonials and happy stories from past clients, he had misgivings, fears, and doubts that this plan would work. So every day for over three weeks when he sat down to begin, Monkey Mind got in the way and he realized doing the work would take more energy than they had imagined. The Hero's Journey for this client was getting stopped right at the Border when the Vision was being brought forth into Physical Reality. Our client tried on his own to "power through" the Monkey Mind chatter of doubt, worry and fear. He found himself at the end of the day with the truth of not having done what he said he would do. He was suffering mentally and physically.

One secret to quieting that Monkey Mind conversation when you're taking steps on your Hero's Journey is simply to be willing. Willing to hear the chatter, observe that you are hearing it, tell the truth and see that the chatter is merely proof you are up to something big… and decide to take action anyway, nevertheless. You might even say out loud "thanks monkey, here's a banana, go enjoy it while I do what am here to do". With this client we discussed all the reasons why a FSBO might use an agent and what services they would find beneficial. The client re-discovered that he had a lot of benefit to offer that would have the owner actually thanking them for calling. He got very clear on what he was going to say, what he could offer that was helpful, and prepared follow-up letters in advance. We acknowledged that some owners might be having their own Monkey Mind conversations about real estate agents too and designed a plan to make the initial contact both short… and sweet for both of them.

Take One Authentic Action

We then recommended that he make the first Authentic Action step small and sweet also. The client was willing to make just ONE contact a day to a FSBO… and ask them one simple question. Designing small sweet steps is another way to keep the Monkey Mind at bay - we simply tip-toe past the monkey, over the border by making it so small that monkey doesn't scream. Our client's Monkey Mind calmed down considerably since it was "just one contact a day and just one simple question" with no expectations on initial results. We also set up weekly calls for mentoring, accountability, and problem solving during this time and Step Three of the journey was under way.

After two weeks this client discovered that the monkey was much quieter and better yet, the people he was contacting said "Yes" to the simple question almost every time. This opened the conversation to other questions and he was able to provide service and knowledge that both truly helped people... and helped them to get to know him. After three months he had listed three new homes from this method of lead generation, and was confident that the additional 12 deals would come about by just getting to three additional contacts per day. The client was a Hero taking powerful Authentic Actions in the final step of his Journey and was bringing about the "great value" that this journey intended. Even better, he now knew he could consciously control his income by simply adding a few more contacts a day.

What a heroic journey he took! Courageous steps and being willing took him through the journey. He turned his visions and dreams into physical reality and overcame challenges, doubt and worry and fear. Out of these challenges, he accepted a mentor's assistance and did the work, both contributing to others who needed help with their expertise, and helping himself to grow both financially and toward his Life's Intention of being a loving parent.

You too can take this journey… and indeed, you are starting right now. To get a copy of a Life's Intentions Inventory, ask for one via email at LII@YourCoachingMatters.com.

ABOUT THE AUTHOR: *Mike and Donna Stott*

Mike and Donna Stott started selling real estate in 1980 and 1986. After incredible careers in residential real estate (peaking with over 180 sales and $2.7 millions in gross commission income) they manifested a big change in 2006 and moved from Hawaii to Atlanta, and started their careers as coaches. Now certified by the Academy for Coaching Excellence and the International Coach Federation, they support over 60 clients achieve phenomenal income while living extraordinary lives.

Their company, Your Coaching Matters, is instrumental in helping agents "stuck" at one level to a breakthrough, as well as coaching those starting out (or needing to re-start) into a full-time, full-paying real estate career. Their clients average $227,000 a year in income! A favorite role is helping agents up their minimum standards so they can make the same, or even more income, with fewer sales.

Their courses include Zero-Resistance FSBO's; Zero Resistance Expireds (with Kate Vail); Profiting from Your Database; Buyers

Mastery, NLP I-III (with Donna Fleetwood); and Building a Successful Real Estate Team (with Kate Vail), among others. Contact them at: Donna.Stott@YourCoachingMatters.com or Mike.Stott@mac.com.

Chapter 15

Invisible – So It's Not Powerful? No Way I Say!

By Alison J. Kay Ph.D.

Wow! I can't believe - I mean I can but - you're such a perfect model of how I teach the mind body connection works! I mean we've cleared out your sixth chakra of its dysfunction and now no more allergies. We cleared out your second chakra of those way deeply held blocks, and now your hips are finally not tight for the first time in years!"

"I know! And not to mention my rocking sex life my husband is so grateful for! And you're forgetting about all the work we've done on my third chakra and getting me grounded from the work on my first - right? Because what about my thriving new business doing what I love AND finally getting my raise - bigger than any of us had expected - AND my decision to go for that refinanced, better mortgage rate that resulted in me now MOVING back to my dream home?!"

We looked at each other, her on the massage table and me looking down at her, each glowing with glee and excitement. Both Chloe and I are yoga teachers. In fact, that's how we met. She waited outside the studio's door as my students and I wrapped up our class, with her students for her Ashtanga Yoga class. Ironically, my certification is in Ashtanga Yoga from India, yet I was teaching a Core Strengthening Yoga & Meditation class that I designed based on mind body fitness, that the yoga studio owner renamed to "Chakra Yoga" due to my holistic approach and the increasing demand for it.

Chloe though, in those first few weeks upon my opening the classroom door, seemed a bit withdrawn from me. Gradually, as I began to greet her, she opened up. I would find out later that at first she was a bit scared to interact with me, telling me she was intimidated by me, to my surprise, but she would correct my understanding, assuring me it wasn't that I was intimidating in my nature, but it was her predisposition to be intimidated by my balanced, centered presence and all that I'd done with my life, because that was what she most desired for herself. Little did she know at the time - but she would later - how many hard choices I'd made and how much I'd done to get there!

Back in the healing room's space, I held her smiling

gaze and said, "You know, it's quite amusing to go into the yoga studio and see all the students and employees and fellow teachers - basically all of them - wearing one piece or another of your brilliant stone creations!"

Chloe laughed, "I know! It's fun! Remember when I could barely keep up with the orders?" This was a whole different Chloe than I had met when we first began talking.

Three months earlier, she had said to me after yoga class one night, "If you can heal my second chakra, then…" Chloe's voice trailed off, as her eyes looked at me with a mixture of hope, excitement and guard-edness, while we stood there outside the closed yoga studio discussing her starting to see me as a client. "Yeah?" I looked at her, opening up the space for her to feel comfortable to share more.

"Oh yeah. I've been working on this for the last year. What you say in class about the second chakra, each time we get ready to tone for the second, and then after, I can feel how blocked I am there, and I know everything that you talk about that is contained within the issues the second chakra covers are mine. My hormones have been off my whole life. And that's just the start."

I looked at her carefully, feeling into the sense of whether she was really ready to let go into a new, better version of herself. Apparently, she was!

"OK Chloe, why don't I text you with an appointment two weeks away? I'll check my calendar and on Monday I can reach out to you and book you in for the following week's opening. Will that work?"

She looked relieved, and her body's posture relaxed in her shoulders seeming to sink down a full inch, as she said, "Sure! Sounds perfect."

We stood there looking at each other, each thinking her own thoughts - and not - but just being there, in this new energy, as we recognized that we'd now be getting a whole lot more intimate.

Chloe came to my healing studio two Tuesdays later, having cleared her busy work schedule as a project manager, trainer, and analyst for a major, international accounting firm. She filled out the requisite paperwork and off we went, with me starting to do a clearing and activation of her pineal and pituitary glands, the two master glands of the endocrine system. "So what did you mean when you said that you've had your hormonal system entirely out of whack your whole life?" I asked.

"Well, my periods have always been hugely painful, with massive, debilitating cramps and outrageous PMS. I've been using hormonal creams for years to help balance myself, but my PMS is still out of control, as are my cramps. And I'd love to not need to use the creams anymore. I've been using these for decades."

She went on to tell me later on in the next session that when she first got her period, it was around the same time that her dad was having an affair and so her parents separated and her life was never the same. Once I did clearings on the trauma in her second chakra and the unconscious blocks there through the hands-on energy medicine weekly sessions over the next three months, eventually, her painful periods gave way to completely manageable ones - but that was not without the first one in the midst of focusing on this chakra being one of the worst she'd ever experienced! Overall, it seems that the trauma of it all - her little child mind had absorbed the energies and concluded in the irrational way our subconscious tends to, that somehow her periods and bad things are connected, specifically with her dad, and perhaps even connected with men. It was simply just too much for her to absorb all at once.

Yet after this healing, she began to speak her mind more to her dad. He even reached out and called her, and initiated more intimate conversations than ever before. I love when that happens; when we make a shift in ourselves, how people who we've had difficulty with previously, end up also shifting when it was us who had shifted! This "stuff" is so cool! And it makes life so much easier and more enjoyable, yes? I also found that her third chakra seemed like it had been splattered; as I wrote in her file: "as if short circuited, fried, taking in too many energies." It did eventually clear of the deep pattern of putting others first before herself and absorbing their energies as Chloe was highly empathic. Yet her third chakra remained quite buried, and used to being inactive, almost dead for her. This did not surprise me for two reasons. First, because she had packed on extra weight there - eating a lot of sugary foods and breads in order to protect the area of our body that seems to really absorb others' energies. Second, that her second chakra had been so shut down, due to her not ever feeling like it was ok to feel what she actually felt, and being shown that her feelings didn't matter. And THAT didn't surprise me because she'd had to grow up so soon, taking on a parenting role for both her younger brother AND both of her parents, as they went through the separation, then divorce, then post-divorce changes. This apparently included even Chloe's mom complaining to her about her father missing child support payments and asking Chloe to ask her Dad for the money. So she didn't have a solid foundation, making her not grounded, leading to her being overly intellectual, and in the head a lot.

What's interesting is this frequently leads to someone being overly reliant on their intellectual abilities, and "in their heads." Yet Chloe was aware of this tendency, and managing it through her meditation practice. And indeed all of her jobs had her in the banking industry, relying much more on her left brain, analytical skills. It was not until she began training others, did she bring in more right brain skills. We worked quite a bit on her feeling safe to open up to her right brain side of herself, the more intuitive self. It's typical in our society; we prove our worth on what's valued - our intellect - and we shut down what doesn't seem valued - our intuition, right?

What also seems to accompany this type of energy pattern - the way our unconscious beliefs have us unconsciously conclude we must behave, and the way this then effects the corresponding chakras, and the way this then effects us in our bodies - is a head that is ripe for sinus congestion. In the holistic model of the mind body connection, an energetic congestion leads to a physical one. This is the premise behind acupuncture, in fact. And it has deeply informed the way I deliver my energy medicine so that people can have more ease, joy, comfort, health, vitality and longevity in their bodies, not just in their minds and spirits.

The effect releasing one's emotional and mental blocks has - let's say once the chakras are open and balanced and flowing energy through, having released the old shut down energy patterns - on the levels of vitality a person has still continues to titillate me. Time and time again, once a regular client of mine has released a certain chunk of their old "issues" or "baggage" they report to me that they have a lot more energy. And I observe this too, through the increased spring in their step, or the presence and fullness they have when coming into the healing studio.

How does this work? "Chakras" translate from Sanskrit into English as "wheels" that flow this "vital life force energy", or prana (Hindu Indian) or chi (Taoist Chinese) throughout the body along lines named "nadis" (Hindu Indian) or "meridians" (Taoist and Traditional Chinese Medicine - TCM) that function as the "highways" distributing - or not - this vital life force energy throughout the body, from the main "city centers" - the chakras - or not, depending on if the chakras are open or closed.

These wheels - chakras - are either opened and turning out the vital life force energy, distributing it through the body region the chakra is located, and thus the body thrives, or the wheels are shut down, closed, and not turning out this virtual life force energy, yielding congestion, or less life-giving regions of the body, ripe and vulnerable for pain, chronic conditions and eventually possibly even dis-ease, or illness.

What is understood in the science of the chakra system to keep these wheels turning out healthy life force energy (think life adding, or life giving) or closed and not turning out this vital life force energy throughout the corresponding region of the body are our beliefs. Each chakra is responsible for a particular domain of life. The technical way to explain this is if we have blocks in our beliefs, then now according to the science just reviewed of the chakra system (interestingly, most ancient cultures had some form of the chakra system, including the Mayans and Cherokees, to name just two) these blocks correspond to certain chakras in the body.

Now the third chakra is key to manifesting; it contains
- all chakras have the sense of having some "right"
- "the right to desire what it is we desire." So if this
seat of the third chakra is at the start of our digestive
tract's fire, at the solar plexus, which is the start of
the intestinal tract, where the stomach empties into
the small intestines and the digestive process begins
to be more strictly metabolized, then clearly, if we are
absorbing too much of others' energies and they are
disturbing - you got it, our digestion can be disturbed.
Each chakra also has an element associated with it,
and the third's - perfectly - is fire. The third chakra
also involves our self-esteem and self-confidence and
joy for going out into the world and manifesting what
we desire. It is considered in the chakra system to be
the seat of our will. So it's perfectly fitting that its ele-
ment is fire, right?

Chloe's fire for herself, and her right to desire - and
manifest onto the physical plane - what she envisioned
for herself and her life had always been suppressed.
The environment her parents created for her had her
more busy with others' energy and needs and feel-
ings and desires, instead of her own. Another aspect
of this seems to be that because she'd been shown her
feelings didn't matter, the only time it seemed "safe"
or "right" for her to express her emotions was during
her period, specifically her PMS symptoms - hence it
was always so bad.

As it happens during the course of sessions with a
client, as we begin to remove the top layers of what

is suppressing the chakra fully expressing itself in an open and balanced way, and we get to the deeper, more buried, denser "stuff" the client has reactions as this buried "stuff" comes to the surface as its on its way out of the body. Chloe was no different. After we began to open up both her second and third chakras, she had a huge blow-out week with her period in the second month of working together with weekly sessions, had the severe headaches she had been used to getting when menstruating, and flew into a rage unlike she could really remember, which was catalyzed by her husband saying something about her belly being puffy - due to menstruating – and he poked her right in her third chakra and she exploded. Yet today, Chloe has secured a near-thriving relationship with her husband. I am in celebration of all the changes this brave, wise, loving woman has made, as she goes about her new life with nothing wrong, creating her best life ever! Om Shanti - "peace" in Sanskrit.

This information about chakras is from Anodea Judith's brilliant work.

ABOUT THE AUTHOR: *Alison J. Kay, Ph.D.*

Dr. Alison J. Kay is a Holistic Life Coach, India trained YA RYT-200 Yoga and Meditation teacher, ACE Certified Personal Trainer, and energy healer/clearer of 18 years nicknamed "the lightning bolt" due to the power of her energy healings and clearings with clients around the globe. The lightning bolt nickname could also correspond to her enthusiasm about what she does. Her students and clients and listening/reading audience say that Alison is able to bring together disparate parts, including making the Eastern holistic philosophies fully digestible, linking what is usually separate in a way that is accessible, understandable and fully connected for the Western mind.

Alison lived in Asia for 10 years. She has been a meditator for 21 years, teaching it for 18. Also a vegetarian, an endurance athlete, weight trainer and yogini, Alison's unique blend of credentials, use of multiple modalities, and the wealth of experience she acquired during the 10 years she spent living in Asia studying subtle energy health and longevity systems, make her perspective and manner of working with people around the world incredibly powerful.

Her work is unique, truly helping to catalyze shifts in people that they didn't even know were possible. The most frequent response Alison hears: "I haven't felt like this since I was a kid!" In other words, when the world is magical and anything is possible! This occurs because Alison lives from an entirely different perspective, attuned to the unlimited possibilities present in consciousness, and with eyes that see clearly how the physical is trumped by consciousness, so if we work with our thoughts, beliefs, emotions and subtle energy then we can create the lives we desire! She has a proven success rate with her clients using this approach that is 99 percent.

Now residing in Florida and frequently traveling and leading sacred health and yoga tours, people from around the world receive her clearings and healings in distance and in person one-on-one sessions and her ever-popular Tuesday night group Theta-Healing™ calls, where folks join in silently, kick back and receive clearings for whatever it is up for them ready to be cleared and lightened, then re-listening to the recording, creating much more light, space and ease in their lives, so they CAN create the life they desire. People also enjoy Alison "Chakra audio Healing Series" with approximately 15 minutes of instruction on each chakra and then 45 minutes of clearings for each chakra. You can go to her site and see what issues correspond to which chakra and choose to clear those issues for yourself with the mp3.

She recently released her first book, written in her last year of the ten she lived in Asia, from Hay House's Balboa Press, "What If There's Nothing Wrong?". "Manifesting Change" is the second book where she is a featured author. She also just completed two years of a radio show she created and hosted that was in the top ten on her network - her ever insightful show, "Create Your Best Life Ever! What else is Possible?" on World Talk Radio, the biggest online media company, at voiceamerica.com. Visit www.AlisonJKay.com to learn more.

Chapter 16

Change, for God's Sake

By Roxann Bauerle

I have spent a lifetime trying to manifest change in my life for what I believed to be for my greater good. It felt like no amount of positivity, affirmations, or hard work did the trick.

I think I got manifesting confused with working my ass off to make something happen. That is what I called Change, for God's Sake! That is a pattern that lasted a lifetime, until now.

What did work was my deep passion to know the Source that was responsible for all the material and non- material things I wanted in my life.

It was through my journey to know that Source that taught me how to manifest deep and lasting change in my life. That is Change for God's Sake.

These are five lessons from that journey.

Lesson #1 — Recognize what is not working

Since I was little, this is what I believed about creating change in my life:

- If I try hard enough, I will succeed
- If I win, I will feel great
- If I succeed, I will experience freedom
- If I make more money, I will feel secure
- If I find the love of my life, I will be content forever.

I was desperate to learn how to enjoy a healthy and long life that had depth and meaning outside of striving for something outside of me. I had a deep interest in spirituality and wanted to focus on what really mattered in my life.

My lesson was to recognize what was no longer working in life and prepare myself to follow the call of my heart and learn a better way to create lasting change in my life. I used this formula that deepens all of my learnings: Identify the lesson; Define the knowing; Inquire within; Take action; and Affirm.

Lesson - Recognize what is not working in your life and be receptive to changing it for good.
Knowing- Be open to the callings of your heart.

Inquiry - What do you really feel called to change in

your life that will create lasting peace and happiness? What is no longer working in your life?

Action - Make a list of the areas in your life that you feel strongly called to change.

Write down what changes you would like to make and define the circumstances that would need to be in place to support those changes.

Affirm – I am receptive to the good fortune that is mine and I acknowledge and accept it.

Lesson #2 — Respond to the Call for Change

I have spent a lifetime of changing for what I believed to be for my greater good.

I believed that if I tried hard enough, I would succeed, if I would win, I would feel great, if I succeeded, I would feel loved, and if I made more money, I would be happy.

Many of these patterns of behavior and beliefs were born out my early desire to be seen, heard, and loved. I believed that if I did all these things to change and succeed, I would feel all the things I so deeply yearned for – love, acceptance, and happiness.

It never happened.

Well, maybe for a short time, but it was fleeting. It seemed to make me hungry for more and so the "cycle" began. The cycle of changing for good and trying hard became the theme of my life. While it served me well in many areas of my life, it left me feeling empty in others.

When life was good, I felt happy. When life was bad, I felt sad.

In times of trouble, my sense of contentment would instantly disappear and I would find myself doing whatever I could to avoid what was disturbing me. Deep down in my heart and soul, I knew there had to be a better way. I would ask myself, "Are we expected to live our entire lives with the our peace and happiness dictated by our outer circumstances? How much do we have to change before we actually feel this love, freedom, peace, and prosperity we yearn for? This can't possibly be the entire purpose of our lives here on earth. What do we have to do to bring lasting change and happiness to our lives?

I was desperate to learn how to enjoy a healthy and long life that had depth and meaning. I had a deep interest in spirituality and I wanted to focus on what mattered in my life.

My dark secret was that I really wanted to know God and how God could help me create lasting change and happiness in my life so that I would not be so affected by emotional ups and downs.

So, my spiritual journey to find true and lasting change began with the three-letter word, God.

Lesson - Stop looking to outer circumstances to determine your happiness.

Knowing – What we need for lasting change is within us.

Inquiry – What is no longer working in your life? What old contracts do you have with yourself that no longer serve you? Do you wish for you life to be different?

Action - Sit quietly and be open to the shifting of your beliefs so you can make room for the change you desire to occur.

Affirm – I speak only words of truth and see them manifest in my life.

Lesson #3 — Three Letter Word for Lasting Change: God.

Those three little letters can potentially bring up of feelings of judgment, joy, anger, disbelief, or confusion. I understand. I can barely utter the word God without feeling judged, scared, frightened, or insecure.

I am not referring to God in a religious sense. For sake of clarity, I wish to define God as I experience it. It is the universal spirit that gives us life. It is an infinite potential that is full of love, grace, peace, joy, and contentment. It is not separate from us.

It is a one Source known by many names; Universal Spirit, Maker, Infinite, Soul, Absolute Being, Holy Spirit, Universal Life Force, Infinite, Creator, or All Powerful. It doesn't matter what you call it.

It is the one thing in our life that is changeless.

I have always yearned to experience it, know it, and let it be a guiding force in my life. I just didn't know how, until now.

Lesson - God, as I know it, is the only thing in my life that is changeless.

Knowing - There is one source, known by many names. It is not separate from us but within each of us. Inquiry- What is the source of all living things? What beliefs do I have about God? How can I have a better understanding of how we are connected to this big thing called life?

Action - Inquire into your definition of God and spend some time in contemplation of what it means in your life.

Affirm – I acknowledge that I am a spiritual being.

Lesson #4 — Know your life has purpose

We are here to learn, grow, be expressive and prosper in all ways. It is all part of the your divine destiny. This is our purpose.

You are given exactly what you need to transform your life. You just have to realize it, recognize it and believe it to be true for yourself. You KNOW it, but maybe you just don't realize it.

The deep longing that you feel for love, the quiet voice within that keeps knocking at your hearts door, the relentless drive to be "somebody", are all signs that we are called to change for God's sake. The answers you seek are not outside of you. They are within.

Go there to begin your journey.

Lesson – I am here for a reason.

Knowing – What you feel called to grow, expand, grow, manifest, and boldly express yourself, it is this great energy of infinite potential. Trust it. You must rise to meet its expansion within you. Give it room to breathe, express, and manifest in your life. It cannot help itself from expanding. It is in the very nature of its being. It just needs you to recognize it, cooperate with it, and nurture it.

Inquire - Contemplate the possibility of your life

having a divine purpose. What is it? What do you feel called to do? What changes do you wish to manifest in yourself and your life? How can you align with this great source of abundance, prosperity, joy, and love? Inquire, contemplate, and be open to the possibility that what you deeply desire is already waiting for you. Develop a strong sense of determination to know this truth.

Action - Act on the knowing of your deep inner guidance. Write down what it is you truly desire in your life. How do you want your life to matter? What do you wish to do that makes a difference in the lives of others? What do you care most deeply about? What is it you wish to manifest in your life that is the fullest expression of who you are? Write it down and read it often.

Affirm - "I want to change, and be better. I want to live in my highest self – and I will."

Lesson #5 — Accept Change, and your Life changes

Change is woven into the fabric of our lives. It's inevitable. It is part of our evolutionary process for good. The more we accept it, the greater impact it can have on our lives.

There are three types of change that we can experience in our lives:

1. Change that we resist, that causes us to suffer.

2. Change that we don't understand that causes us to Surrender.

3. Change that we accept that causes us to Transform.

Change that we resist, that causes us to suffer exists because we cling to ideas, beliefs, and situations that we deeply desire in our life.

We feel we really want them in our life and we will stop at nothing to make sure we get them. Our determination or circumstances drive our decisions and we become blind to a situation that might not be right for us.

Our stubbornness, inability to let go, and fear of change, keep us stuck. Often times, we endure physical, emotional, and spiritual pain as a result of our resistance. We are left feeling angry, annoyed, upset, tense, afraid, confused, sad, tired, lonely, and hopeless.

In short, we suffer.

We blame others and circumstances for our situation. We cling to old beliefs and ideas that keep us stuck. We experience it unconsciously and begin to believe that our entire happiness is dependent on outer circumstances and situations.

This is a formula for continued suffering. This cycle continues in our life because we don't look deep enough within our own heart, mind and soul to challenge and inquire into our ideas, beliefs and situations that keep us in this pattern of suffering.

I can't quit, no matter what

I took a job because I had an idea that it was going to be a perfect fit for me and the money was good. Who has not done that, right?

Deep down in my heart, I felt a strong resistance that I ignored. On the first day of the job, I had a deep strong feeling in the pit of my stomach. I said silently, "I made a mistake."

I ignored this feeling for two years because I made a commitment to accomplish the goals of the job and I was determined not to leave. I believed, "I can't quit, no matter what. We need the money. We can't survive without my income. I am scared to pursue what I really love." These thoughts kept me in a job where I felt terrible. Toward the end, it got so bad, I would cry on my way to work. I knew on a deeper level that I was there for a reason and this job was part of my journey. For that reason, I accepted it and did my best. It was when I repeatedly ignored my feelings that it was time to leave the job that caused me to suffer. I was ultimately let go from that job.

When I was let go, they asked me what I would like

them to tell the staff. I said, "Tell them my work is done." You have to know when your work is done. When do you stop resisting and move on in your life? If you check in with yourself and inquire deeply within, you will know exactly what you should do. Listen, to the still small voice within and trust it.

That job was a critical part of my spiritual journey and I don't regret it. I suffered because I was so resistant to the "knowing in the pit of my stomach" that it was time for me to move on. I resisted that knowing with every ounce of my being and I suffered greatly.

That job experience was the catalyst to go out on my own and work for myself. I didn't know that at the time. The letting go was making room for what I wanted more of in my life; freedom, peace, joy, and independence to pursue what I love and believed in. In hindsight, I don't know that I would have left that job on my own, no matter how much pain I felt. So the firing was blessing in disguise.

I often say, "It's the universe's way of helping a little girl out, when she can't help herself."

I have learned to tune into the compass of my soul with greater awareness, and my life is free from suffering, because of it.

Know - Tuning in to the compass of your trusted inner voice, having faith in a power greater than yourself, and quieting your mind will help you minimize your resistance to change. Get still, quiet, and listen within.

Inquire – Contemplate the idea that change is happening for a good reason. Ask yourself, "What change am I resisting in my life that is causing me to suffer? What areas of my life do I feel called to change? What is it that I fear about change? Can I accept that change is natural part of my life? Can I let go and let God do the work"?

Act – Follow your heart. Is there something is your life that you know you should be change but have not done it? Take one step today to make a small change toward making room for more of what you truly desire in your life. The more you "free up" your energy toward resistance to change, the less you will suffer. The less you suffer, the more room you create for lasting and meaningful change in your life.

Affirm – With your strong will affirm, "Established in God awareness, I am poised and peaceful."

Change that we don't understand that causes us to surrender exists when innate knowledge wishes to unfold within and it manifests itself in circumstances or situations that we do not understand. Some unplanned events in our life are fortunate and others may be troublesome or cause discomfort or pain.

It is as though we are being released from the bondage of conditions we do not want in our life. My experience was just that.

Fear of the Unknown

It was Friday, and I was sitting at my office. My heart began to beat so fast I could actually hear it. I was finding it hard to breath and my chest felt very heavy. The fear began to run through every cell of my body. I felt like I was having a heart attack.

I thought, "What is happening? Am I having a heart attack? I am healthy. I work out.

I don't drink or smoke. Why me?

I have not felt a fear like that in all my life. I stood up to ask my assistant to please come in my office. I lied down on the floor to try and catch my breath. She called the ambulance and they decided to take me to the hospital.

My body began to shake uncontrollably and my teeth began to chatter. I couldn't control it. This was the first time in my life I had ever felt these feelings. Completely helpless and surrendered to what wanted to come out of my body. It was not something I was used to, at all, trust me.

I felt scared about my health, shame for needing help, and vulnerable because I was not in control. After a series of tests, they determined that I did not have a heart attack. It was an anxiety attack.

The attacks continued for over two years. It seemed like an eternity to endure the fear they brought up in me. I felt like I was going to die every time I experienced them. They forced me to experience and surrender to vulnerability like I never had before. I felt as if I was at the hand of something so much greater than little ole me.

I had to just brace for the ride. Determined not to take any medication to suppress them, ignore them, or prolong their inevitable return, I endured their storm. I had no other choice but to learn how to surrender to their unpredictable uprisings in my body. Surrendering was the only way out. I would breathe deeply and not let my conscious mind get scared. I stopped trying to resist them and opened up to what they had to teach me. It was one of the hardest things I had to do but the greatest release of fear I have ever experienced.

I experienced a deep sense of peace and absence of fear when the attacks finally stopped. It taught me that changing for God's sake is surrendering to that which keeps a veil over our true essence of love, peace, and joy. If we are unconscious, we can't see this essence in our Self.

Life has a way of creating change in us that we don't always understand, but it brings us great freedom in the end.

Know - Life's greatest blessings can be experienced in

the darkest of times if you surrender to them. Surrender to the change and open yourself up to the greater blessing that wishes to transform in you.

Inquire - Contemplate the idea that the greatest challenge you face in your life could be the most significant step in transforming into your highest and best self. Ask yourself, "Are you experiencing change in your life that you don't understand? What could it be telling you? What would it feel like if you embraced it with full abandon?

Act - Embrace the change that is manifesting in your life with courage, faith, and love. Trust in its ability to transform you. If you know the change is for your highest good, let it take the place of great fear. Face the change with full abandon and surrender to this change in your life. You might marvel at what is on the other side. Trust the process, it is a blessing in disguise.

Affirm - "I am fully committed to rapid awakening through the remaining stages of my spiritual growth. I am strong, fearless, and confident."

Change that we accept, and causes us to transform exists when we have finally surrendered, accepted, and understood why change in our lives is necessary and realize that it is all part of our evolution in realizing the God that lives within each of us.

I suffered greatly in my life because I did not want to

accept some of the circumstances that were happening in my life. No matter how bad I felt, there was nothing I felt like I could do to change the external circumstances in my life. What I could change was how I responded to them.

When my son was nine months old, I got divorced. My family lived in another state, I did not have a job, and I needed a place to live. I felt scared, disheartened, and humiliated. It was one of the most challenging times of my life. It was heartbreaking and I felt tremendous guilt. I always told myself no matter how difficult it got trying to maintain an amicable agreement with my ex-husband; I would do what was in the best interest of my son, no matter what.

I had to trust that it would all work out. It was the hardest thing I have ever done. Many nights I would cry myself to sleep and pray that I could transform my feelings of anger, resentment, and helplessness into feelings of peace, empowerment, love, and trust. Eventually, those feelings did transform. I let go of resisting and accepted what I could not change. Additionally, I had to have faith in something bigger than me that it would all work out.

I learned to transform the thoughts and feelings that kept me stuck. I moved from feeling angry to acceptance, fighting back to letting go, and controlling to having faith. I desired to change myself so that I could stay at peace.

I controlled the thoughts in my mind that created my personal hell while accepting the situation and all the people involved. It was a long process, but one of the most transforming ones of my life.

Lesson - When I have thoughts, feelings, regret, or sadness about my past behavior or circumstances, I examine them and come to terms with them, then discard them or transform them.

Know - I can remain in soul contentment in all circumstances.

Action - Ask yourself what you are not accepting in your life? What are you deeply resisting? Notice it, pay attention to where it feels in the body, then breath into it.

Affirm - I know myself to be an agent through which God's power flows.

These lessons have taught me that our entire lives are a journey of change.

Change, for God's sake is understanding how we can use change in our lives to connect to a greater purpose. It's about learning how to stop "trying so hard" to create the change you desire, but giving way to an "effortless surrender."

It is a deepening event that occurs when we shift,

lay aside, or abandon ideas, beliefs, and experiences, that keep us unaware of our true God Nature and our infinite potential.

It is a process that includes, replacing our beliefs, removing the blocks that hold us back, and abandoning that which does not serve our highest good.

It is about transformation. Transforming our old beliefs, habits, and experiences of Truth.

It is remembering and aligning with the Universal energy that wants to be expressed in each of us.

It is about being an instrument for this energy of love, peace, prosperity, joy, and abundance to **express through us.**

Once we do that, all that we seek to manifest can flow through us and to us.

When we Change for God's Sake.

ABOUT THE AUTHOR: *Roxann Bauerle*

Roxann Bauerle has realized that real change – the kind that leads to healing, bold-self expression, transformation, and unleashed potential requires dedication, curiosity, vulnerability, and strength.

After 15 years in corporate America working for companies like NBC, Clear Channel, and Comcast, she knew there had to be a better way to balance work, life, and her passion to help others so she founded the Inspire Marketing and Coaching Group.

Roxann runs inspired life and business programs, and helps entrepreneurs create authentic and mission driven brands. Her programs combine spirituality and business. Their blend of wisdom and practicality make her work deeply meaningful and effective. It is her mission to inspire greatness in women around the world so they can live the life they love. She is a marketer, author, speaker, and certified life coach. She lives in San Jose, California with her husband and son.

Conversations with Curtrice:
Empowered Abundance

By Curtrice Goddard

The pathway to abundance and the creation of a life designed from an infinite point of view is through vibrational alignment. This is a conversation about taking all the tools and teachings we have acquired on our spiritual path and looking at them from a broader perspective, from the perspective of vibrational alignment.

Vibrational energy is what takes a fool-proof strategic plan, a structure, or a system and provides it with the energy to manifest and work for you in accordance with what you desire. Have you ever wanted to create something in your life or seek results that someone else has achieved in their life, business, relationship, or health? You follow the how to's only to fall short of the success you are seeking? Well, there is a powerful component frequently left out of the equation. This is the component of energy. You cannot create the big dreams of your life unless you are energetically vibing at the same frequency of that dream. It's not about only what you desire, it's about the energy of what you desire and do you match that? Ahh, yes this is the question of the day.

So, knowing this, isn't it logical to focus on how you are vibing? What is the overall essence of the energy you are consistently emitting? Answering these questions will explain to you how you are creating what you are creating in your life.

Humans are dual, we are both physical and spiritual beings, and while much of life's focus is on the physical, the application of mental understandings, hard work and action the soul and energetic part of us can go out of focus, left untouched or put as a last priority. I am eager to share with you the power and complete significance of focusing and navigating your vibration as you create a life you love! Focusing more on your energy is a game changer.

You may be wondering what is vibration? Vibration is simply the energy you are emitting at any given moment. It is the accumulation of your thoughts, intentions, words and beliefs. You can find the nature of the vibration when you ask yourself the question "What am I sensing and feeling here in this moment?" It's a powerful tool! If you inquire within yourself, what energy or vibration am I emitting right now, you'll know the answer by how you are feeling. If you are feeling inspired and joyous, you are in a high vibration; if you are feeling depressed and fearful or stressed, you are in a lower vibration. These are two ends of the spectrum, neither are wrong or right however it's good to be aware so that you can consistently and lovingly focus on staying within a high vibrational range.

The invitation here is for you to become aware of how to manage your vibrations and begin to live and create a life from this platform. We are energetic beings and vibrational frequency is in fact shaping our life. It is what is creating the reality you are experiencing at any given time. Everything you want is in the higher vibrational range. All you perceive as good is easily obtained and experienced when you are in higher vibrations more often. The less desired outcomes reside in the lower vibrational range.

I figure if a person knew that all creation (manifestations) are vibration before they are tangible actual manifestations, one would live with a focus on how they are are vibing, right!? This is the opportunity to flow through life with more ease and knowing. We are creators, calling things into being through thought, vibration and choice. We are shaping our lives and expanding all the time. Life is not happening to us, we are happening to life. It can be very comforting to sit quietly and reflect on what it means to be a human being, a part of all there is, it is not a small thing at all! We were born in all of God's glory, we are a unique version of God. We were born equipped to live on this earth in joy and in empowerment, even through life's challenges.

I have created 7 Degrees for you to achieve and maintain a high vibrational state of being. Knowing that this is where true navigation of life resides, having these tools and methods to live will serve you well. In this chapter I go through a few of the degrees, and I will share with you how to tap into more of them at the end of the chapter.

7 Degrees to Empowered Alignment/Abundance

1.The presence factor (living in the now)

2. Perspective shift (shift happens!)

3. Embodiment (Live the energies of your dreams realized)

4. Mental nutrition (daily focus)

5. Meditation your way (self-nurturing time)

6. Movement, play and dance (shifting & releasing stagnant energy)

7. Soar in high vibration (enjoy being a confident creator, live the dream)

I consider these degrees gifts, they have assisted in transforming my life and have supported me in creating a joy-filled life from an expansive place. I have experienced personal profound transformation using these degrees. I offer them to you with the intent for you to discover within yourself your own knowing, power and wisdom and for you to better understand and consciously work with the creative process of life.

1. Live in the now

You hear live in the present moment a lot but what does it truly mean? Our point of power is always in the now moment, right now is when you can make choices for change. It's the opportunity to gain clarity and it is in the now moment where you can connect in deeply with yourself, ground in and become present.

Presence should not be underrated. In the world of creation, this is a very powerful aspect. Whenever we are in the past, we are focusing on what is no longer (things we cannot change and/or re-live)and of course your future outcome is subject to what you feel and choose in the now moment so the now is in fact our most precious and powerful moment.

As you are reading this, are you here now or are you thinking...carried off into a thought? Bring yourself back to the present. Feel your body, sense your breath, feel the seat you are sitting in. Become present to your now and see what insights you gain. If you are feeling any stress about the future, release your thoughts and ground into the now moment. In this moment all is well. Right here, right now.

If you are experiencing a challenge in your life, a great question to ask yourself as you use this tool is, what is TRUE for me right now? What is true in this now moment without judgment and conclusion of what you think is going to happen in the future. Here are a few examples where the now moment has helped me transcend ego limitations, fear, anxiety and has supported me into becoming a powerful conscious creator.

When I was terminated from my job of 13 years abruptly, it was a shock and a shift! For the most part I was fine with it, I've always sensed that one day life would eventually shift for me into a scenario where I could create more and live out my divine purpose. I didn't know what that would look like, I didn't know it would show up in the form of a termination. As a person who lives on purpose, I knew on a soul level termination was my gateway into MORE, more of me, more of doing what I am passionate about, more love, more money, more, more, more!

Even with this understanding and deeper insight, days rolled around when the path seemed unclear,

I slipped into habitual fear-based thoughts of doubt and fear, worried about the future, what will happen, I thought, what if this doesn't work out like I dreamed? Even thoughts about survival, how will I eat? The unknown was scary! It was momentary insanity, I call it! I call it insanity because none of it was true in the now moment. I hadn't lived my future yet. It was an unwarranted freak out! Yes, sure there were pressures present with no income coming in, court dates with the ex-employer who contested my unemployment, rent due and a few other circumstances arising and even though I've always known on a soul level that I am a prosperous, whole, amazing self -realized entrepreneur, I allowed myself to begin to think fearful thoughts like "How do I start my own business? How will I do it all??"

This was all just fear, fear, fear, blah, blah, blah. I was far from being in the now moment. I was way into the future and creating fearful outcomes while I was at it. It is these type of situations when the now moment will bring you back to you, back to knowing, back to a place where you can see clearly and hear the guidance that is always with you. You can hear the truth. I asked the question, "What do I know right now?" Not a day from now, not next week, what do I know right now? Instead of focusing into the future possible destruction, like oh my rent is due, etc., I became present and what I knew in the now moment was all is well, I have plenty, I am sure, I have been and will always be guided, I can breathe here. I released and allowed life to show up without my conclusion. Conclusion is limited and it feels heavy. Possibility and the unknown is vast and plentiful. In the now moment all things are possible. Opposed to how will I do this or that, I released the future, I released the past of what occurred to get me here and I listened to the now moment. This allowed my vibration to rise to one of hope and helped me shift out of the lower vibration of fear and stress. Like I said earlier everything wanted is in the higher vibration.

The now moment was and is so steady. It is full of "all is well right now" and it is full of allowance for infinite possibilities. You have all you need right now. It was a powerful shift for me to look around and see what I had in the now. I had plenty, and I became OK with not knowing the future.

I know the not knowing aspect of living is uncomfortable as our personality/ego self wants certainty of outcomes. However, we are speaking to and calling in our highest self, our God self, our infinite beingness and approaching life from higher perspective, this way of thinking is transformational and getting you where you want to be. You have to be OK with the ego not knowing everything. Let's be OK with allowing the soul and higher knowing to lead as you integrate your ego self and follow with trust, faith, love and joy and your heart.

When you ground into the now and sense all the well-being there, clarity and the soul's reassurance arises within you. From this place, your mind is open to receiving, your heart is open to receiving, you literally open pathways for resources and insights to find you. You are clear and massive stress resides, you become lighter and more of your true self, the empowered self. From this place you are empowered and ready for the next moment from a serene and steady place. This will allow you to do more, to feel more vibrant and you will see your solution come into form. ALL your power is the now.

2. Perspective shift! (Shift happens!)

This is my favorite degree! I create so much fun in my life utilizing this degree. One of my favorite quotes is Dr. Wayne Dyer "Change the way you look at things and the things you look at change". You can even challenge yourself with the question, "How can I make everything I do fun!?"

This gives you all the power in your life. No one and nothing can determine how you will experience anything because you have the power to shift it! You can shift your perspective towards all things. Anything from the most mundane tasks, to a job you hate, a relationship that is dragging or a flat tire you can always, find a positive more fun or at least a lighter way to look at it. This will instantly boost your vibration and when practiced keep it in the high vibing spectrum.

When we are experiencing a challenge in our lives, it's easy and habitual to feel defeated, frustrated, scared or any other emotion that doesn't serve the vibration of ease, joy and knowing. The expected response to a less than desired situation is to feel "Oh crap! Why me? It's always something" or to go into scarcity and fearful thinking. When you become aware you are doing this, changing your perspective will free you from feeling constricted, will free up limited thinking, and you get to choose a lighter more expansive way to view things.

I'll share a perspective shift that brings me to how I am even writing this today. When I was working at my corporate job, I lost interest as I began to evolve and feel into my sacred life's work. I was attending Naturopathy school for natural medicine, I had adopted and cultivated spiritual practices and I even began helping close friends, family and my co-worker's with their health ailments. I was in my groove and enjoying it.

I fell in love with natural medicine and it's all I wanted to do. I would light up when talking about it! I found even at work, my day would consist more of talking about holistic health than the duties required for my job. Did I want to be there? No. I was seeing my life unfold in such amazing ways outside of work, and my job in the accounting department within a casino was no longer fitting for me. I felt the need to expand.

Here is where the shift comes in. Perspective truly is everything. I never complained about my job. In fact I did the opposite. Despite the inner revelations I was having. I praised the job! In order for me to love the new life emerging within me, I didn't have to bash the old. I kept my thoughts about it steeped in appreciation. I would feel gratitude for everything from the pay check to the bagels. I enjoyed my co-workers, It was a love fest! I chose to make it a love fest, my vibration depended on it. I found appreciation within it all. I made it work by shifting my perspective.

My commute to this job which no longer resonated with me was over an hour, I would use this time to listen to motivational, inspirational CDs and my favorite music as well, music from artists living their passions, inspiring and uplifting. I listened to CD's that reminded me of who I truly was! I was jamming! By the time I would get to work I was on fire and filled with joy! I radiated love even though I was working in a place I no longer wanted to be. How's that for vibrational living! This is what true perspective shift looks like. I was high vibing! I knew my vibration is what mattered most and the black and white tangible reality focus was futile.

I had to shift vibrationally in order for things in my life to shift to what I truly wanted. It's such a win win because the perspective shift made me more attractive, happy and peaceful. I was able to inspire others and be a contribution to all I encounter there. Even though I was still going to my desk job every day I knew in my heart one day I would be an entrepreneur, a best-selling author and an inspirational speaker, I just knew it! Vibrationally I was already there.

Remember, now is the only moment we truly have, so in the now I was in high vibes cultivated by shifting my perspective. Applying this to every aspect of my life helped me to create a life I love. My life began to shape up in a way where there wasn't anything present in my life that I didn't want to do. If I didn't want to do something at first I would shift it!

As I said earlier, I was eventually let go from this job and I was terminated on a day when I was very happy, feeling invigorated and joyous and because I was consciously applying the 7 Degrees that I teach. I knew whatever was to come after the termination had to match the high vibing frequency I had been emitting, and boy did it ever! I found a certain calm in knowing I had been consistently nurturing my vibration so no matter what things LOOKED like, I knew vibrationally it was all coming together perfectly. This gave me confidence in how things were evolving.

The ending of my corporate desk job became how I come to write this now and share my heart, gifts and message with the world. Yes, my dreams and goals at that point have manifested and is continually unfolding! This is the life of empowered abundance and it shows how living from an vibrational standpoint can help you create your dream life.

Disclosure: "People around you may not understand or relate to your responses to life when you have adopted a vibrationally focused lifestyle. You are calmer, more sure and relatively happier even when challenged. This way of living may set you apart for a while but you will eventually be able to shine, give back, inspire, actualize your dreams, have peace and be a total contribution to the people in your life and to the world."

Please join me for the remaining 5 degrees and begin your vibrational journey to creating your dream life with ease and joy! Join our community for game changing tools for living from your empowered truth and creating an abundant lifestyle! Choose, align and create!

ABOUT THE AUTHOR: *Curtrice Renae Goddard*

Curtrice is Holistic wellness and lifestyle consultant, an inspired speaker and teacher. She facilitates transformational workshops rooted in conversations about consciousness and expansion as a tool for inspired living. She is a joyful energy worker, who believes strongly in the inimitable human spirit. In Conversations with Curtrice, she shares how you can transform and manifest your dream life through practical applications of the universal laws.

Visit www.curtricerenaegoddard.com or email Cutrice at curtriceg@gmail.com

Chapter 18

Seven Steps to Happiness

By Erica Glessing

I am blessed to be a naturally happy person. Over the last few years, I have transformed the very landscape of my life. In the process of experiencing massive transformation, I was given gifts to share with you on how to experience more happiness each day.

As I go about my waking day, loving most moments, feeling joy each and every morning when I wake, my happiness stems from seven basic practices that I live, breathe and emulate. I teach happiness because I get that it can be elusive. I've written over 800 original happiness quotations because they are given to me from source to share with you. I teach that the key to happiness can be tricky – and it changes all the time. People ask me "What is your secret?" and I tell them, when I can, when there is an opening for me to share.

Being open to happiness is the first step, and a lot of what follows is a discipline of happiness. Here are the seven steps to happiness that I practice in my life:

1. Let go of resistance to what is

2. Stand in your own light

3. Believe in your ability to be in perfect co-creation of the life you seek to experience

4. Love yourself: past, present and future

5. Forgive yourself and everyone in your life for everything

6. Focus with solid intention on your choice of thoughts, feelings and emotions

7. Connect to universal, source or celestial God energy

Create a Happiness Journal

To chart your journey on the seven steps of happiness, begin with a journal so you can amplify your happiness and manifest change in your life with ease, joy and grace. I spoke with a woman that I have coached on happiness for about three years. I have seen her become so joyful in her life. Of all of the teachings we have worked through, she said that keeping a journal of happiness, wins and gratitudes has been profound. So start today. Journal your wins, your gratitudes, and what makes you happy. I personally am in deep gratitude that you have found this book! I am feeling happy because more people are connecting to happiness in their waking moments.

Now for the seven steps to happiness, and manifesting everything you desire in your life.

Let Go of Resistance to What Is

When you look at your life as a co-creator, you can be gentle about what you like and don't like in your life. You can let go of resisting the landscape of your life. It is possible you have a desire for a more beautiful relationship with your family, or a more perfect car, or a better house, or maybe you would like your career to take off in a new direction. It could be there is a book inside you that is not born yet. Whatever your desires may be, one of the keys to happiness is to allow yourself to have a desire to be more or better while not being in resistance or in criticism of your present experience.

One tool for letting go of resistance is to ask yourself to let go of resistance. Happiness is here, where you are in complete beauty in your life regardless of what your eyes or seeing or your hands are touching.

Ask yourself "what is right about myself and my life right now?"

Ask yourself "is today temporary? What else might show up today?"

And as you let go of resisting all that is around you – as you trust that you made decisions with the best intentions, and you can make new decisions right now – happiness may find itself sneaking into your life.

This is just the first step!

Stand in Your Own Light

When I work with people who are seeking a new job or about to go on a job interview, I ask them to write three pages of things that are good about themselves, and three pages of accomplishments from previous jobs. Then no matter the question that shows up on the interview, the person will be prepared with something good to say about themselves in each of their past positions.

When you allow yourself to see your own light, everyone in your life gets happier. When you feel good about you, everyone else can feel good about themselves.

Take a moment now to recognize three things about you that are special, amazing, beautiful or right. For me, I can say that I am a gifted writer, I am a gifted teacher, and I am a gifted mom. Notice that you may feel uncomfortable when you are standing in your own light. Notice how you may have been raised NOT to compliment yourself, or stand in your own light. In fact, you may have been raised to seriously list all of your shortcomings so you can work on them. Ugh! Take a moment right now to list 10 things about you that are really wonderful. Can you cook a pizza from scratch? Can you match colors in a room, choosing beautiful art for the walls? Can you write a poem? Can you sing in a choir? Can you walk a mile? Begin with some extraordinary things but then notice some ordinary things that are also special. Do you smile when others walk in, brightening their day? Are you a good listener? Can you speak rap music? What is deep and genuine and true about you?

You want to really get into this step, and get through anything uncomfortable about it.

I love the word JUICY lately. What is juicy about you? When do you feel joy? Riding a horse? Riding a dolphin? Riding a motorcycle? Riding a skateboard? Riding in a fast car? Riding in an airplane? I'm playing with you here to delve into this step more deeply. I'm going to talk for a moment to those people (and I have worked with you before) who are stuck right here. Some people simply do not believe there is anything special about them. Some people are so hard on themselves, they do not need enemies.

So first, I want to let you know that I have great news for you. You are special intrinsically because you have a soul, a spirit, and a beingness that is 100 percent truly your own. You cannot "NOT" be special. That is, you are special because you are breathing, alive, and belong here in this time and in this body and as you read these words, stand in wonder. Look at your thumb. I'm not joking. Stop and look at your thumb, because not one other person on the entire planet has this thumb. Not one other person was born the exact instant as you with your hair color, eye color, genetic past, spiritual past, geographic past, and orientation as far as destiny (future). So just be in awe of yourself right now.

Is this selfish? Is it somehow wrong or self-centered to stand in awe of one's own being?

On the path to waking up happy, and sharing joy and happiness with others, self-love cannot be underestimated. Go through this exercise for the purpose of seeing what might change in your life when you get how powerful, amazing and great you are.

Write down a few more things you like about yourself, now, if you can. If you have a stuck feeling about words, draw a picture of your smile or your hand or your hair or your body. Write down something someone said about you once that was good.

If you are already feeling like you get this, grow it and expand the feelings a bit bigger.

Expansion Exercise

Stand with both feet on the ground and lift your arms up to the ceiling and stretch

See your energy filling up the space about a foot around you in all directions

Now see your energy filling up the room you are in

Now see your energy filling up the house or building you are in

Now see your energy filling up the city you are in

Now see your energy filling up the country you are in

Now see your energy expanding to the entire globe
And now see your energy expanding to the entire universe and all of the galaxies

Now relax and come back to center and breathe deeply
And bring your energy back around you about a foot in every direction

And ask the space around you to be sacred, and blessed, and filled with the joy of your own expansion

Do this once every morning to set the arena for a fabulous day.

Know You Are in Creation of Your Experience

This is one of the most exquisite happiness steps, and I really can't get enough of this one. This is about knowing with perfect and complete expectation that when you change your energy, your beliefs and your actions, you are in creation of a new world around you.

This is where the joy comes in.

This is where your life shifts into the next level, then the next level, then the next.

As you stand in belief of your ability to change the course of your life instantaneously, you own your power. And as you own your power, happiness is an energy you can feel, breathe and experience more fully and more wholly.

The purpose of this entire book, quite actually, is to awaken your own belief that you can manifest change in your life. Transformation is possible and probable and is in fact happening all around you at all times.

Since you are changing all the time to become more of what you are thinking about and believing and acting upon, you can consciously direct these changes to be in harmony with the vision you hold for yourself.

Change your vision for you.

Let reality be a little less clear and a little more blurry around you.

As you see yourself experiencing the truth of your own power and beauty, your life has the opportunity to unfold in great expansion, joy and deliciousness. New experiences begin to show themselves to you.

You will find yourself bringing out the best in others.

You will find that people will enjoy working with you. You will find that synchronicity begins to be a way of life.

When you are in conscious co-creation of your life, and you are choosing certain practices, your life can flow into alignment with the "new" ways of being.

When doubt and fear and old patterns show up, take time to tap into your greater knowledge and live your new truth.

Love Yourself: Past, Present and Future

A popular song my kids are singing relates to the omnipresent "monster in the bed, the voices in my head." And the song asks for help on how to quiet those voices, and how to live clear and clean without the monsters surrounding you. Getting into loving yourself REQUIRES letting go of dismissing perceptions of you that are not truly about you.

I know that likening loving yourself to housecleaning doesn't sound very sexy. Yet, true pure love is at the heart of every person. You are capable of fully loving yourself, when you let go of the ties that bind you to other ways of seeing yourself. It's like cleaning inside your house, letting go of all that no longer suits you. Light streams in when you let it in. Light can't always get through grime, dirt, or past negativities that you may cling to as a way of feeling comfortable, or normal. Unless your childhood was one of solid bliss where the adults loved and cared and gave to you unconditionally, you may have a few places where you can clean and clear judgment from the space around your heart, mind, soul, body, spirit and being.

Let's begin today. See yourself being loved unconditionally and offer this to yourself right in this moment. Glimpse where you are perfect. Glimpse where you are exceptional. Where are you light? Where do you feel joy? Touch this place inside of your being that longs to shine.

What prevents self love?

Our brains are built to keep us functioning, and our brains can also serve up road blocks. What thought is keeping you from feeling joyous in this very moment? Take a moment to write down some of the views that people had about you that got stuck inside of your self-percept. Write them now!

Now take a moment to write some aspects of yourself that are fabulous, exceptional, spiritual, loving, kind and amazing. Here are some aspects of me that people have always loved: my creativity, self expression, sweetness, optimism, and my intuition.

Can you make a list of good things about you? Can you make a list where you are standing in deep connectivity to the very greatness you are. I challenge you to step into this bigger, right now.

Words You Can Say to Awaken Self-Love

What is beautiful about me?
What is amazing about me?
What is right about me?
What is gifted about me?
What is inspirational about me?

I personally believe that all of you here right now reading this passage are gifted, and have a lot to give. As you seek, so it is shown. As you ask, so it is answered. So trust you are reading this passage for good reason and you are beginning to awaken to the love that is all here for you, all the time.

Forgive Yourself and Everyone in Your Life for Everything

Whenever I have moments free, I go through my life and I forgive more past experiences. When you forgive, you are healing yourself. I was reading a story about a famous man who was sick for several years after he was shot, taking a bullet in the back. The bullet was not removed after the shooting, and no one knew it was inside of him. It made him sicker and sicker. Then when the bullet was removed, he was able to regain his health.

Now, as he was being poisoned by this bullet, what was happening to the man who shot him? We may not ever know. But the poison of the bullet was killing the person carrying the poison – that's a lot like what happens when you carry poisonous thoughts about someone from your past.

I teach forgiveness so that we may free ourselves from these bits of poison we carry around towards others. Holding back from forgiveness kills ourselves, not others.

Once you commit to forgiveness as a way of being, so many new pathways and opportunities will show up for you. You regain life force, and you regain happiness, you regain much of what you lost by staying in a place of not forgiving.

Some of the people that you could take time to forgive, in your master plan, may include parents, teachers, spouses, children, aunts, bosses, employees, strangers who harmed you or your family, pastors, and anyone who gave you something awful that you accepted and sucked into your being.

I give you permission, in this very instance, to open yourself up to complete and total forgiveness to your past, present and future.

You don't have to know how right away, and you don't have to know when it will happen. You don't have to do anything yet. Just for this moment, stand in the concept of forgiveness and ask your spiritual self to connect to "all is forgiven" as a way of being. Forgiveness happens when you actively forgive, however. So once you stand in forgiveness, you can learn exactly how to forgive.

Is forgiving condoning?

One thing I like to teach right off is that forgiving is not condoning. How do you forgive unforgiveable acts? I take us back to the knowledge that "not forgiving" is going to bring about sickness, and carrying around poison is not good for our beings. So connecting again to the pathway of being in forgiveness being the path to manifesting the best life for ourselves, we get a little less attached to who we have to forgive or how we are going to do that.

Know that each person is experiencing choices, and each of us has a say in what we experience. So let go of whatever allowed you to experience an unforgiveable act. And in this now, in this present, be healed and be of great joy that forgiveness is here inside of you. Release that person from your life.

Forgiveness as a daily way of being

Once you forgive, you may have to forgive again. I remember when my mom died in 2003, and one thing about her passing shocked me. I thought I would only remember the beautiful moments of her parenting me. I thought I would be filled with a life stream of beautiful memories, one after the other, when she taught me art, and respected my writing, and loved my intuition, and all of those things that we shared that were great.

But it wasn't like that.

When my mom died, I was shown where she hurt me, where she was wrong, and where her fixation on aspects of my being were so much a part of what is wrong that it was almost unbearable. One memory I have is the "breast reduction pamphlets" she began to send me when I was in my early 20s – until my 40s when she passed.

Now we shared so many beautiful connections, and I love my mom's spirit to this day. But there are some things I need to forgive her about, and her dislike of my body is one of them. As I forgive her inability to accept my body, and her attachment to liking my body when I was about 11 or 12 (before I became a woman), as I let that go, I can be healed and strong and accept my own shape and form for all that it is and all that it isn't, without judgment.

Forgiveness may not be easy, but as you stand in this light and beautiful place of being connected to your greatness, forgiveness is a cornerstone of becoming all that you are possible of becoming!

You can learn more about my forgiveness teachings at www.HowDoIForgive.me. I feel so strongly about forgiveness I built a video series around it.

Focus with solid intention on your choice of thoughts and emotions

Here's where the manifesting of a new life, the transformation process, can get sticky. Because when you are not focusing with solid intention on what you would like to experience, you shift into the automated patterns that built you the life you have now.

I'm guessing your life is much better than it was at possibly a lower point, and may not be all that you would like it to be. As you experience desire for more love, more light, more money, more freedom, more passion, more of everything you came here to experience, this desire burns in you a passion that makes the transformation possible.

Passion and intensity of focus gives you the power you have been seeking to change your life.

When you are not clearly focusing with solid intention on your choices of thoughts and emotions, you are being wagged like a puppy by history, neural pathways, patterns, habits, and people around you that may not get you have an insanely wild and incredible side of you that is just aching to be born.

So many things can take you out of your zone. I just like to remind myself (and people who follow me) that it is indeed my zone, and not anyone else's zone. As

I stay in that place of loving, peace, kindness, compassion, and joy, as I stick to the higher place where I know so many things are possible, then I am rewarded with being shown how very much is possible. And the power to create whatever it is I wish for in my life. It is this constant discipline of shifting into what is working, and to shifting my focus into what is right, that gives me the power to change my life.

And the tendency will almost always be to focus on what is not working, and on what hurts, and on who is to blame.

As you take back your power, you will be able to attract great new people into your life to reflect your beautiful new ways of being. You will feel things flow easier, and you will be able to manifest change in your life nearly instantaneously.

You become someone that everyone would like to say yes to – because you are just that much fun to be around, and because you know how to get things done. Becoming a powerful manifesting individual is good for you, and good for everyone around you. Here is a tool to focus on what you are seeking in your life. Take a moment now and write a one-year prophecy letter for yourself. Write this in the present tense. Write a list of accomplishments and satisfactions from this year as though they were completely finished and complete.

Connect to Universal, Source or God Energy

Transformation flows easiest when you connect to universal, source or God energy. Happiness flows easily from this space. As I write this I am so joyful. I am so blessed to have a connectivity to source that flows into me and through me, and guides my waking moments, and helps me with creative solutions to problems that may emerge in my life.

Here is what can be amazing about getting connected: the way to get connected is not the same for every single person. I remember a fabulous couple, and each teaches how to connect to God. This is their full-time passion and how they make a living, too. One chooses to meditate at length. The other person connects all the time easily from anywhere. She just stops and connects. They were having an argument. He wanted her to meditate for longer periods of time. I laughed with her on this. I said you connect with God when you are washing the dishes. We both started laughing.

She knew in an instant what she had always known, that for her, it was a simple ask and then it was given. For him, connectivity would emerge upon a quiet time of meditation where all thoughts were silenced and the pattern of supreme connectivity could be invited. For him, there was a ritual involved, and this was the very best way to get connected and ask questions of God.

Your way will belong to you. It will feel like you and smell like you and it will be easy for you. Will it be easy for you to heed the messages? That is another question! I have another friend who couldn't get connected. We looked at her life. She loves to ride bicycles and run long distances. I said that perhaps that was her meditation. When she is running, the thoughts flow in, and it feels very pure, and she can ask any question.

I invite you to explore the questions about when you feel connected. And develop a practice, a commitment, an honoring of this higher part of you, and allow that to come into your life in the means that best suits your life.

I believe that you can be guided by the light of God. For me it happens when I am playing basketball. I go down to the gym, and I choose times when it the gym is close to empty. I start shooting around and my body relaxes, and no other busy thoughts are messing with me, and I am not checking email, and I am not on my phone. In those moments, I am given such bright and brilliant insights. I feel so blessed to be able to connect to God and the energy of all that is in this manner.

I do love meditation. I love quiet moments. I believe firmly in having unplugged times when you are not at the beck and call of any human being or electronic device. But I also wonder if you might need to lighten up about it. Because you can turn a song on the radio and hear God's voice, and you can see a leaf fall from a tree and be in awe. Celestial energy is here for you, and you are a truly special part of all that is.

Being All You Are

You already are all that you are. So you don't have to do anything, be anything, prove anything, get skinnier, get healthier, get married, get divorced, get a job, find a business, to become all that you are. You may desire more things and more experiences and that is beautiful and life energy pouring through you.

But just as you are, right now, you are beautiful and I am blessed to have you reading this story.

ABOUT THE AUTHOR: *Erica Glessing*

Erica Glessing began to write professionally in high school, and never looked back. She was a news reporter for over a decade with more than 5,000 published articles. Her book *Happiness Quotations 365* is being published in 2014, as a sequel to her book, *Happiness Quotations: Gentle Reminders of Your Preciousness.* Erica believes that when you tell your story, you change the world. By expressing yourself, you may heal one person, or you may bring light to one life. She started the company Happy Publishing to publish authors with strong stories to tell. Find out more at www.EricaGlessing.com or www.HappyPublishing.net and enjoy her original daily happiness quotations at www.Facebook.com/HappinessQuotations.

THE END

CPSIA information can be obtained at www.ICGtesting.com
Printed in the USA
LVOW10s0634110614

389412LV00001B/1/P